T0065367

POST-TRIBULATION AND THE TWO BEASTS OF REVELATION

A Historical Approach to Revelation

WAYNE GRANT

WESTBOW
PRESS®
A DIVISION OF THOMAS NELSON
& ZONDERVAN

This book is a work of non-fiction. Unless otherwise noted, the author and the publisher make no explicit guarantees as to the accuracy of the information contained in this book and in some cases, names of people and places have been altered to protect their privacy.

WestBow Press books may be ordered through booksellers or by contacting:

WestBow Press
A Division of Thomas Nelson & Zondervan
1663 Liberty Drive
Bloomington, IN 47403
www.westbowpress.com
844-714-3454

Unless otherwise indicated, all Scripture quotations are taken from the (NASB®) New American Standard Bible®, Copyright © 1960, 1971, 1977, 1995, 2020 by The Lockman Foundation. Used by permission. All rights reserved. www.lockman.org

Scripture quotations marked KJV are taken from the King James Version.

ISBN: 978-1-6642-1951-9 (sc)
ISBN: 978-1-6642-1950-2 (hc)
ISBN: 978-1-6642-1952-6 (e)

Library of Congress Control Number: 2021901603

Print information available on the last page.

WestBow Press rev. date: 1/29/2021

DEDICATION

To the Lord Jesus Christ and to all who love His appearing

I hope this book will inspire you to keep studying the scriptures and waiting for the day of Christ.

He gives strength to the weary, and to him who lacks might He increases power. Though youths grow weary and tired, and vigorous young men stumble badly, yet they who wait upon the Lord will gain new strength; they will mount up with wings like eagles, they will run and not get tired, they will walk and not become weary.
—Isaiah 40:29–31

CONTENTS

PREFACE

After I wrote this book, I was reminded of the book of Joshua and the entrance of the sons of Israel into the land of Canaan. The conquest of Canaan took only six years, but each step was triumphant, beginning with the fall of Jericho. Only once were they defeated, and that was at Ai, but God turned even that into a victory. I was adding up the battles, and the record was about 31 to 1. This impressive record reminds me of the victory we have through our Lord Jesus Christ.

Another interesting fact is that when the Israelites crossed the Jordan, it was during harvest, when the spring rains caused the flooding of the river. This speaks of the Holy Spirit. Now, when they entered the land, God had already provided food, since it was harvest, so He did not muzzle the ox while it was treading the grain. We are approaching a similar battle to the Israelites. The tribulation causes fear in the hearts of many people, and I think this is because we have been fed a wrong view of the tribulation. Not to say it is easy street, but we must not fear the waves that are under the feet of Christ (Psalm 46).

But when I look at the conquest of the land by Joshua and the Israelites, I am reminded that our inheritance is certain because of the finished work of Jesus Christ. This is His land because He bought it with His own blood. As we harvest souls for Christ, we cannot be defeated. Satan and his angels have been disarmed by the cross of Christ and, like the kings of Canaan, they know their time is short.

Knowing how severely God dealt with the Israelites in their first attempt at the land, Joshua must have been completely fixated on not coming up short, as before. He and Caleb had been denied the Promised Land because of the bad report of the other ten spies and the unbelief of the older generation. This time was going to be different. This group had faith.

So, as we approach this time, we need to look again at what God has done for His people in the past and move out with renewed courage. We can recall the sound of the seventh angel who blew the last trumpet and announced, "The kingdom of this world has become the kingdom of our Lord, and of His Christ; and He shall reign forever and forever" (Revelation 11:15). The end is already announced.

What is significant about the land of Canaan is that, according to Genesis 15:18, there were ten nations in Canaan. Joshua then was about to overthrow these ten nations. Jesus Christ is about to defeat the ten nations represented in the feet of the image of Daniel 2. Now it says, "In the days of those *ten* kings the God of heaven will raise up a kingdom which will never be destroyed" (Daniel 2:44).

What a great time we live in, and I know that we, together, will do great things for our God.

INTRODUCTION

I heard an interesting sermon on John 6 on the feeding of the five thousand. The point was whether we, like the little boy, are willing to surrender our meager lunch of five loaves and two fishes into the hands of Jesus in order to see a harvest of souls. Our human efforts can never feed a multitude, but when we surrender what we have to Christ, then God can use our gifts to feed many. Even what we have is a gift because we no longer live, but Christ lives in us, and not I but the grace of God in me, as Paul says. So here, I offer this feeble work into the hands of Jesus Christ and ask Him to use it for His glory.

I wrote this book because the time of the end has drawn near. We know that prior to the Second Coming of Jesus Christ, the Bible speaks of a seven-year tribulation period, where great upheavals take place and difficult times fall upon humankind. Jesus said, "We must work the works of Him who sent Me as long as it is day; the night is coming when no man can work" (John 9:4). This period we are talking about is called the night. Christ is the day; Antichrist is the night. Christ represents spiritual life; Antichrist, spiritual death. One is light; the other, darkness. The night is coming. This is when darkness has authority for three and one-half years, when Antichrist reigns upon the earth. This is a time of the persecution of Christians much greater than we have experienced in the past. Other signs are mentioned as well, such as pestilence.

The COVID-19 pandemic is just a reminder to us of what can happen in a short time. But the first sign Jesus mentions is not pestilence or persecution but deception. Jesus says, "Take heed that no man deceives you. For many will come in my name saying 'I am Christ' and shall deceive many" (Matthew 24:4–5 KJV).

Deception, then, is where we need to begin. Today, we have a great amount written on prophecy. But Jeremiah 23:21–22 says,

> "I have not sent these prophets, yet they ran; I have not spoken to them, yet they prophesied. But if they had stood in my counsel, and had caused my people to hear my words, then they should have turned them from their evil way, and from the evil of their doings."

Jesus said, "And many false prophets will arise and will mislead many." (Matthew 24:11).

Prophecy should lead the church to repentance and to returning to the Lord. Most of the prophetic books coming out of America today promote the pretribulation rapture theory. However, many simply state their pretribulation view and still discuss the Olivet discourse, as warning to the church. Others, in order to support their dispensational positions, exclude the Olivet discourse as spoken [1]to the Jews and not the church. The pretribulation rapture theory, unfortunately, has become one of those deceptions.

Another deception prevalent today, and more to the text, is the identity of Antichrist. Jesus is saying, "Take heed that no man deceives you. For many will come in My name saying 'I am Christ' and will deceive many." The particle *for* gives the reason or cause of the deception. This is the present deception about Antichrist. Let no *man* deceive you. Stop allowing yourself to be deceived. The Reformers believed the Antichrist was a historical figure, but most prophetic books today look for a future Antichrist, not a historical one. These writers are, not surprisingly, closed to a post-tribulation rapture as well. Jesus's first sign corresponds with the opening of the first seal in Revelation 6:2, where a rider on a white horse appears. Both this rider on the white horse and the many saying "I am Christ" are the same Antichrist. (This will be discussed in more detail.)

In this book, I attempt to give evidence from scripture and other scholars on what the Reformers have always said; namely, that in the

---

[1] Unless otherwise indicated all scriptural references will be from the New American Standard. (Holman: 1976)

papacy, we must find this man of sin, the son of perdition, who exalts himself above every so-called God or object of worship so that he takes his seat in the temple of God, showing that he is God (2 Thessalonians 2:4).

I also attempt to show, as many others have said, that the futurist view of Revelation has its source not in the Word of God but in the counter-Reformation, beginning with a work on Revelation by the Jesuit Francisco Ribera in 1595 (Wikipedia, "Francisco Ribera"). Ribera taught that Antichrist could not be the pope because the book of Revelation speaks only of a future Antichrist at the end of time. This man and others of the same persuasion set out to undo the claim of the Reformers that the pope is the Antichrist, the man of sin, the one who takes the seat of Christ.

But the papacy has claimed to be the vicar of Christ since the late fifth century (Wikipedia, "Pope Gelasius I"). The pope, alone, claims to be Christ on the earth, something no political leader has done or is doing. Therefore, the many who say "I am Christ" are the many popes.

The key text the Reformers used for their claim was 2 Thessalonians 2:4, where the apostle Paul describes the Antichrist as the man of sin who sits in the temple of God, claiming himself to be God. The Greek word for *temple* in 2 Thessalonians 2:4 is ναος. The noun ναος is always used for the temple of His body, the church, and not the physical Jewish temple.

But the word for the physical temple is το ιερον. It is used twenty-five times in the book of Acts, but not even once is this temple called ναος. In John 2:19, Jesus said, "Destroy this temple and in three days I will raise it up." This temple is *naos*, and John explains that Jesus was speaking of the temple of His body. This temple is the church of God. The Jews misunderstood which temple Christ was talking about, even today.

Therefore, just based on this text alone, we can for certain identify Antichrist with the one who now sits in the church of God as if he were Christ. This has been the seat of the papacy since the sixth century—not a brief sitting in a reconstructed Jewish temple that doesn't exist, as the futurists claim, but in the temple or church, as if he were Christ, the head of the church.

There is no greater deception than this—to pretend to be Christ so that people worship you instead of Christ. Equally as misleading is this counter-Reformation scheme which attempts to cover up the true Antichrist by deliberately creating a false scenario. How do we know which pope will be the final Antichrist? Because each one holds the seat of Antichrist, therefore they are all the beast. Everyone in that seat claims "I am Christ," and the popes have sat there, making them many Antichrists. The seat of Antichrist must hold Antichrist. His seat has been in Rome since the dragon gave the seat to the beast, according to Revelation 13:2.

Some attempt to avoid the tribulation simply by teaching a pretribulation rapture. But this only adds to the cloud and leaves the church vulnerable. Rome is drunk with the blood of the saints already, and many of the souls who died in the Reformation are crying out, even now. Read *Foxe's Book of Martyrs*, by John Foxe, if we should need convincing, but God has His witnesses then and now.

> Surely the Lord God will do nothing unless He reveals
> His secret counsel to His servants the prophets.
> (Amos 3:7)

Certainly, the tribulation time is one of His secret counsels. The present pretribulation rapture theory has its source in the counter-Reformation. This is part of the cloud whether intentional or not. There are two key elements in the strictly futurists position that prove a common theme, even if it is not intentional.

First, they never know who Antichrist is, even though the Reformers washed their robes in the blood of the Lamb, declaring who he is. Second, they do not know when the rapture will be, when Jesus says plainly in Matthew 24:29 that it is "after the tribulation of those days". Both these teachings have a common source and purpose, for most unintentional—to cover up who Antichrist is and leave the church unprepared for the tribulation. This is certainly not our intention as Christians.

I believe, then, that the Reformers were correct in calling out the popes the beast of Revelation 13 and Antichrist. He will come to Israel (rider on a white horse) and make a peace agreement with Israel to allow them to build their temple in Jerusalem. This could be Pope Francis, not because he is any worse than the two hundred or more popes before him but because he sits in the place of Christ. This is how he is identified. Make no mistake: the apostle Paul clearly identifies the one who sits in the church of God, who shows himself to be Christ, as Antichrist. He is the lie, but Christ is the truth. What fellowship has light with darkness or the temple of God with idols?

In 2014, Pope Francis visited Jerusalem and was seen *standing* at the holy place of the western wall of the temple (like but not Matthew 24:15). Was it a foreshadowing of things to come? Kind of like the pandemic. He also wore his *white* robe. Sometimes he rides in a pope mobile. He rides the *white* horse. He came bearing the olive branch of peace, "saying 'Peace, peace,' but there will be no peace." But what does God say to Israel?

> And your covenant with death will be disannulled, and your agreement with hell shall not stand; when the overflowing scourge shall pass through then you shall be trodden down by it. (Isaiah 28:18)

Just like Daniel 9:27 says, the prince will break his covenant in the middle of the week, and his army will trample down Jerusalem for forty-two months (Revelation 11:2). Yes indeed, this is futurism but it is also historical because he presently sits in the church of Christ in the place of Christ. (2 Thess. 2:4)

During the visit in 2014 and recently, there have been discussions between the Vatican and Israel about the future Jewish temple. Remember that to build such a temple, the Jews will need the support of all the faiths represented in Jerusalem—the Armenians, Roman Catholics, and Muslims. Believe me; without the pope, this cannot happen. Make no mistake: we do not deny a futurist Antichrist but equate him with the historical one.

Let's be plain: until we see the temple being built in Jerusalem, there is no final week (Daniel 9:27). This temple, however, as I've explained is not the same temple of God mentioned by Paul in 2 Thessalonians 2:4. He is seen *standing at* the holy place of the Jewish temple in Matthew 24:15 but sitting in the church of God in 2 Thessalonians 2:4.

The purpose of the counter-Reformation futurism was not to warn the church but to hide the real Antichrist who sits in the temple of God right now. This deception will be how the false prophet persuades Israel to accept Antichrist. They will say, "Peace, peace, but there will be no peace" (Jeremiah 6:14b). Peace for Israel comes through the righteousness of Christ in the gospel, not an ecumenical peace mediated by Rome.

The building of the third temple will begin in Daniel's seventieth week, even as the destruction of the temple in AD 70 marked the end of the sixty-ninth week. No one disagrees with a third temple being built.

Before we get into the specific material of this book, I need to present an overview of the two beasts mentioned in Revelation 13: the beast from the sea and the beast from the earth. We can miss the forest in looking at the trees, and so an overview is necessary. In Revelation 17:9–11, John discusses the seven mountains upon which the woman called Babylon sits. He says,

> Here is the mind which has wisdom. The seven heads are seven mountains on which the woman sits, and they are seven kings; five have fallen one is, *the other* has not yet come; and when he comes, he must remain a little while. The beast which was and is not is himself also an eight and is one of the seven and he goes to destruction. (italics mine)

The Greek word for *other* is another of the same kind. This Greek word is used in Revelation 13:11 as well for the beast from the earth; beast of the same kind as the sea beast.

According to a great many commentaries, *these heads* are seven successive empires. The four empires mentioned in Daniel 7 are all called beasts. Four beasts are mentioned in Revelation: the dragon, the beast from the sea, and the beast from the earth and the scarlet beast. The five fallen mentioned in Revelation 17:10, according to these commentaries, are Egypt, Assyria, Babylon, Medio-Persia, and Greece. The sixth empire *that now is* would be the Roman Empire, when John wrote Revelation. Most agree with this.

It is plain, that the beast *that is*, or the sixth beast of Revelation 17:10 is the dragon. When you compare it with the fourth beast of Daniel 7:8ff it is clear they are Rome imperial. The dragon has ten horns, just like the terrible fourth beast. In Revelation 13:2, all the four beasts of Daniel 7 are mentioned. The fourth beast not mentioned in Daniel is identified in Revelation 13:2 as the dragon or Imperial Rome. But Rome had two legs in the image. This is the reason Daniel is so key to understanding Revelation. The book of Daniel is the little book which is now open mentioned in Revelation 10.

The Roman Empire fell in AD 476. But this was just the first leg of the legs of iron. The second leg is Papal Rome and it began when the popes were given *temporal power* in the Papal States in the 8th century. This also included the crowns on the horns the beginning of the Holy Roman Empire.

The first crown was Charlemagne king of the Frank, the new emperor. These kings beginning in AD 800 reigned until 1805 when the Holy Roman Empire was abolished by Napoleon. This is the end of the second leg of the image in Daniel two.

The Dragon and the beast from the sea are the two legs of iron and both represent Rome. But the beast is also an individual just as the popes from the 8th century held temporal power until his temporal power was taken away in 1798 by France. The Pope was removed from Rome in 1796 and died in exile. This is the deadly wound of one of the heads of the beast from the sea. His temporal power was taken away by France two years later.

This head would be healed as an eighth when in 1814 Pope Pius VII took seat in Rome. In 1929 the beast received back temporal power in the Lateran Treaty. The second leg of Daniels image then ended around 1805. Both these legs are iron and represent Rome the sixth head. This is the dragon and the beast of the sea. Notice John's chronology in Revelation 12 and 13. He is expounding the image in Daniel two. Not to recognize this is to confuse what John is presenting in Revelation 12,13 and 17.

The Holy Roman Empire, then, is the beast from the sea. John in Revelation 12 and 13 presents these two legs of iron, the dragon, Imperial Rome and the beast from the sea, Papal Rome. The little horn is the Papacy and is also the beast from the sea.

Both a kingdom with the Holy Roman Empire having 10 crowned

horns and as an individual, Antichrist. Each successive Pope is the head of the beast and this continued until one of its heads had a deadly wound. One of the Popes was removed from its seat and their temporal power taken away. This happened in 1798 and together with the defeat of the last emperor Francis II in 1805, came the end of the Holy Roman Empire, the second leg of iron.

The dragon and the beast of the sea then are both the sixth head. They are identical, having seven heads and ten horns, even as the legs of iron are identical. Each lasted about 1000 years. This picture is key to understanding John's vision in Revelation. Now, according to Revelation 13:11 another beast from the earth will arise. John mentions the beast from the earth as the third beast in his chronology.

So then when the beast of the sea was declining or the sixth head was ending, another head or beast was rising in succession—the seventh head. This must be the beast from the earth, as John places them in this order. If the sixth head is papal Rome, the same head as Imperial Rome, then the beast from the earth must be the seventh head. The beast from the earth emerges but it is not iron, but comes from the earth. This beast must be the clay in the feet of Daniel's image.

Another point is that the beast from the sea has no woman riding on its back like the scarlet beast of Revelation 17. We must conclude then that the scarlet beast in Revelation 17 is the eight beast. What empire emerges from 1798 when the sixth head was wounded? What emerges after the legs of iron come to the end with the dissolution of the Holy Roman empire? Well this must be America, who is recognized as a sovereign nation by France in 1798.

This, is when America begins to rise. She corresponds to the beast from the earth, and is therefore the seventh head. She is the clay in the feet in Daniel's image. She is also the woman Babylon who rides the scarlet beast. America began in 1776 and in 1798 was recognized as a nation.

Napoleon was instrumental in the dissolution of the Holy Roman Empire and in the removal of the temporal power from the pope. Just when the Papacy loses its temporal power and when the Holy Roman Empire ended, America begins. The legs of iron give way to the beast of the earth, the clay.

So then, just when the Holy Roman Empire ends, the beast from the earth emerges as the seventh head. America is recognized as a new nation the same year the sixth head ends. America, then, is the beast from the earth with two horns, like a lamb, but speaks like a dragon.

In 1929, by means of the Lateran Treaty, the Vatican was given temporal power once again. Just like the idol of Dagon was set up again, after it had fallen. It had fallen but was not broken but healed. Vatican City, one of the seven hills of Rome, comprises an area of about 109 acres. Mussolini gave this area to the papacy so that they became a sovereign country again. This happened after the seventh head, or America, had appeared. This is the scarlet beast which is the iron in the feet.

The beast from the sea then is also an eighth head. By the deadly wound the beast was and is not and yet is. Now this is the reappearance of the iron in the image. But where is the clay? The clay is the beast from the earth, the woman who rides the beast.

John is still following the image of Daniel and now in Revelation 17 just prior to **the judgment** of the whore, he shows us the feet of iron and clay. Here is the future alliance of these two beasts.

Like the feet of iron and clay at the end of the image so we see an end time union of the two beasts in Revelation 13. America, we said was the beast from the earth. This is the clay in the image and is the woman Babylon united with the scarlet beast, the eighth head, also of iron since it is still Rome. These two beasts join up at the end. This is the feet of Daniel's image and now revealed by John in the Revelation. To argue that the woman riding the beast is the Roman Catholic Church is not too difficult to refute. John sees this woman just before she is judged. This judgment is in Revelation 18 where Babylon a rich commercial system is destroyed by fire. This is not the Roman Catholic Church.

Also, this woman is called a harlot. The Roman Catholic Church would be an adulteress since she was part of the Church of Christ. Now America has never really been Christian nation, but is a beast from the earth which has horns like a lamb but is really a dragon and speaks like a dragon. She fits with the harlot. She is Babylon.

John calls this sixth head an eighth because it appears after the rise of the seventh head. This eighth head is also the beast, antichrist and makes great boasts and has a mouth filled with blasphemous statements, like saying he is the Holy Father, the vicar of Christ, head of the church, and even the Lord God. This head, or little horn, receives world power in the last three and a half years but only in union with Babylon. America is the power which as the beast from the earth elevates the first beast.

The image in Daniel 2 provides the background for John. The dragon is the first leg of iron, and the beast from the sea is the second leg of iron. After these the land beast appears in chronological order. This can only be America appearing as a lamb like beast with two horns. This is the seventh head. She becomes the clay while the scarlet beast the iron in the feet. Two beasts united.

The Reformers could only see the sea beast since they were living in the iron leg time. The beast from the sea had no woman riding on its back. The second leg is only iron. But they interpreted the woman of Revelation 17 as the Roman Catholic Church. However, they did not understand the feet of Daniel's image. The Reformers were not aware of a beast from the earth because it had not come up yet. We can therefore understand their position, in view of the persecutions they were facing.

But John Wesley in 1754 in his explanatory notes on Revelation suggested the land beast was about to arise. But he assumed it was from Asia. Speaking on Revelation 13:11 Wesley says,

> "Out of the earth — Out of Asia. But he is not yet come, though he cannot be far off for he is to appear at the end of the forty-two months of the first beast." (Wesley, Notes on Rev. 13:11).

Nevertheless, his comments got people looking for what John described as the beast from the earth. As we said the image of Daniel is the key to understanding the four beasts in Revelation 12,13, and 17.

Revelation 18 speaks of Babylon as a rich land with cattle, chariots, sheep, slaves, spices, gold, silver etc. where all the merchants of the earth are made rich by trading with her. Only America, fits this description in Revelation 18. America is also a military power. This is not the Roman Catholic church.

The United States is the largest operator of military bases abroad, with 800 military bases in 70 countries around the world. (Wikipedia: US Military Bases).

Babylon is called the hammer of the whole earth (Jeremiah 50:23). America fits with the beast of the earth and the woman of Revelation 17:3. The beast from the earth has two horns, while the dragon and the beast from the sea both have ten horns on their SAME head. The ten horns identify these beasts with Rome, just as the fourth kingdom in Daniel 7 was Rome.

The beast of the earth is America, because it arises as the sixth beast has the deadly wound. America has two political parties but without any crowns—a democratic republic. America is divided as are the feet in Daniel's image. She is the clay in each foot. It was founded on Christian principles with lamb-like qualities, but in the end is one of the dragon heads. America is the woman who rides the beast. John shows her just before judgment in Revelation 17:1-3.

Here is the feet of iron and clay in Daniel's image just before the stone hits the image and causes it to fall. The iron and the clay are the beast from the sea and the beast from the earth, iron and clay. These two beasts merge into a new world order at the end, just as in the feet. Fallen, fallen is Babylon the Great are both these beasts.

Therefore, this is the reason for the warning in Revelation 18:4: "Come out of her my people that you may not participate in her sins." This warning is given by John, just before Babylon is destroyed by fire— nuclear war. Her fall comes before the tribulation ends, and so there is no rapture. We must leave her when the time comes. Just before the morning comes.

Isaiah 17:14 says, "At evening time behold there is terror! *Before morning* they are no more. Such will be the portion of those who plunder us, and the lot of those who pillage us." Here we have God's plan against the Assyria/Babylonian alliance, which plunders His land and His people.

The beast of the sea is also Babylon, because the two have become one flesh. Revelation 18:2 says, "Fallen, Fallen, is Babylon the Great." Both these beasts will fall, economic Babylon the seventh head near the end of the tribulation. Then the scarlet beast and the ten horns at Armageddon. This is an overview of the premise of this book. These beasts are empires which Satan shall use to persecute the church and scatter Israel.

> "These will wage war with the Lamb and the Lamb will overcome them, because He is Lord of lords and King of kings and those who are with Him are the called and chosen and faithful." (Revelation 17:14).

Let us move on to discuss the final week. The picture with which we will begin our discussion concerning end times is the Feast of Tabernacles. This feast lasted seven days. Tabernacles is the final feast of the year. These seven days, I believe, represent the seven-year tribulation before the end of the age. On the first day and on the eighth day, there was a holy convocation. The Israelites dwelt in tabernacles during the feast.

This feast, prophetically, has not been fulfilled yet and represents the final of the three feasts. in each feast, it was mandatory for all of Israel to participate. I believe that in John 7, when Jesus refuses to go to the Feast of Tabernacles and then appears on the last day, it is a picture of Christ's Second Coming at the end of the tribulation. Even Jesus then will participate in this feast on the last day. Let's look on.

For seven days, the Israelites were to present an offering by fire. The fire is a hint to the tribulation. They also dwelt in tents, but at the end, they tore down those tents and lived in a building. Paul says if our earthly tent "should be torn down," then we have a building from God, eternal in the heavens (2 Corinthians 5:1). Both the Feast of Unleavened Bread and Pentecost involved Christ and all believers. I will not leave you as orphans He said but will come to you.

Therefore, the church of Christ must participate in this final feast as well. Jesus said, "Truly, truly, I say to you, unless you eat the flesh of the Son of Man and drink His blood you have no life in yourselves" (John 6:53). Participation in the Passover is not an option for every believer, nor is Pentecost, for Paul says in 1 Corinthians 12:13, "For by one Spirit *we were all baptized* into one body whether Jews or Greeks, whether slaves or free, and we were all made to drink of one Spirit." We have all drunk of one Spirit at Pentecost.

Therefore, participation in the Feast of Tabernacles must include every believer. Why, then, would the church be raptured prior to this feast, when they share in the other two? And since there are no more feasts after Tabernacles, it must represent the end of the age.

Some might say that these feasts were for Israel alone and not the church. This is the usual dispensational view, but if we look at what these feasts fulfill, then it becomes clear. These feasts were prophetic of the coming of Christ as the Lamb of God, of the coming of the Holy Spirit, and the Second Coming of Christ at the end of the age, just as the sacrificial system was prophetic of the sacrifice of Christ on the cross.

I believe we are about to enter this final feast, the last one. When? Maybe sooner than you think.

> Now on the last day, the great day of the feast Jesus stood
> and cried out saying if any man is thirsty let him come
> to Me and drink. (John 7:37)

When Jesus's brethren urged Him to go up to this feast, Jesus said, "Go up to the feast yourselves, I do not go up to this feast because My time has not yet fully come" (John 7:8). His own people wanted Him to show Himself to the world as the Messiah, but Jesus knew He would have to attend the Feast of Passover in order to be the Passover lamb. Tabernacles was at the end of the age, but Jesus did appear on the eighth day of the feast, just as He will appear on the last day of the seven-year tribulation. Jesus said, I will not drink of the fruit of the vine until I drink it anew with you in the kingdom of God. Jesus participates by His second advent.

1

End of the Age

Let's move along to what the Bible calls the consummation of the age. In Matthew 24:3, we read, "And as He was sitting on the Mount of Olives, the disciples came to Him privately, saying, 'Tell us, when will these things be, and what will be the sign of Your coming and the end of the age.'" Matthew combines the sign of our Lord's coming and the end of the age. In the Greek text, these are indeed the same event. When Christ returns, this age will end, just as He appeared on the last day of the Feast of Tabernacles. The Greek construction—της σης παρουσιας και συντελειας του αιωνος (Your coming and end of the age)—follows Granville Sharp's rule for Greek grammar.[2] This rule is as follows:

> When the copulative kai connects two nouns of the same case, if the article ho, or any of its cases, precedes the first of the said nouns or participles, and is not repeated before the second noun or participle, the latter always relates to the same person that is expressed or described by the first noun or participle.

Simply put, these events combine under one article: *the sign of His coming and end of the age.* Jesus's Second Coming is at the end of the age, not prior to it, as we have been led to believe.

---

[2] All Greek references are from B. Aland, et al., *The Greek New Testament* (XXXX: United Bible Society, 1983).

This end of the age is described in 1 Peter 3:10, "But the day of the Lord will come like a thief, in which the heavens will pass away with a roar and the elements will be destroyed with intense heat, and the earth and its works will be burned up." Indeed, anyone living on the earth at this time certainly would not survive the event described by Peter; hence, the need to be raptured before the wrath of God.

> Behold the Lord lays the earth waste, devastates it, distorts its surface, and scatters its inhabitants. And the people will be like the priest, the servant like this master, the maid like her mistress, the buyer like the seller, the lender like the borrower, the creditor like the debtor. The earth is completely laid waste and completely despoiled, for the Lord has spoken this word … Therefore, a curse devours the earth and those who live in it are held guilty. Therefore, *the inhabitants of the earth are burned and few men left*. (Isaiah 24:1–3, 6 italics mine)

Isaiah says the inhabitants of the earth are burned, just as Peter says the earth and its works are burned up. Even so, according to Isaiah, some men are left, but there are few. Peter adds that Christ's return will be like a thief. This seems to suggest that the world will be caught off guard and unready, as when a thief breaks in when you are asleep. In fact, Christ compares His coming to the flood, but not expecting either cataclysm.

> For the coming of the Son of Man will be just like the days of Noah. For as in those days which were before the flood they were eating and drinking, they were marrying and giving in marriage, until the day that Noah entered the ark and they did not understand until the flood came and took them all away, so shall be the coming of the Son of Man. (Matthew 24:37)

However, Noah and his family knew when the flood would come because they had been preparing for it for many years. God told Noah the flood would come after seven days, like the seven days of the Feast of Tabernacles. These are the seven years before Christ's return. We will know the year, so for Christians, the Second Coming *will not* be like a thief. If we are watching, we will not be surprised. Jesus says the days before the Son of Man comes will be just like the days of Noah. The seven days before the flood in Noah's day are just like the days before the Son of Man comes. The former is prophetic of the latter, even as the Feast of Tabernacles is prophetic of the end of the age. Once again, we have the seventieth week predicted in Daniel 9.

Just as the Lord Jesus stood up on the eighth day of the feast, Noah and his family entered the ark after the seven days—on the eighth. Christ will return after the seven-year tribulation, just as Matthew says:

> But immediately *after the tribulation* of those the sun will be darkened and the moon will not give its light and the stars will fall from the sky and the powers of the heavens will be shaken, and then the sign of the Son of Man will appear in the sky. (Matthew 24:29–30 italics mine)

There seems to be a time of relative peace at the end because Jesus says they will be eating, drinking, and celebrating, just as they were in Noah's day. Paul suggests a false peace and security at the time of the end:

> For you yourselves know full well that the day of the Lord will come just like a thief in the night. While they are saying "Peace and safety!" then destruction will come upon them suddenly like birth pangs upon a woman with child and they shall not escape. (1 Thessalonians 5:2–3)

They will marry and be given in marriage, planting and harvesting with the future in mind. Just like in the days of Noah, the tribulation will not register on them. Or they may all say the seven years are over and nothing has happened, and they may go back to their unbelief, mocking us and saying, "Where is the promise of His coming?" (2 Peter 3:4).

Atheistic secularism does not regard the Bible or the signs. They reason that everything is according to the natural. Global warming is just because of carbon emissions. The COVID-19 pandemic will soon be over, and the world will be back to business—no real discernment. Even today, we have locusts in India, but that is India and not us. These are signs for those who are watching. When the seven years are over, they will say, "Nothing has happened. We told you so." Then, suddenly, like a thief in the night, destruction will come.

Birth pangs precede the birth of the new age.

> For nation will rise against nation and kingdom against kingdom and in various places there will be famines and earthquakes. But all these things are merely the beginning of *birth pangs*. (Matthew 24:7–8 emphasis mine)

These birth pangs are what we call the tribulation. The world only sees this global warming and climate change as man polluting the earth and not as signs of the end of this world. "Things will get better," they say. But Jesus calls these things the beginning of birth pangs, suggesting the pains will get worse. Tribulation will increase.

We hear stories every day of weird weather patterns but now is overlooked as global warming. Mockers in Peter's day made the same assumptions and, like the scientific community of today, refused to believe the biblical account. It's like Pharaoh, who concluded that the plagues of Egypt were not from God—same hardness of heart. No wonder Jesus says, "When the Son of Man comes, will He find faith on the earth?" (Luke 18:8b).

In Hebrews 11:7, it says,

> By faith Noah, being warned by God about things *not yet seen*, in reverence prepared an ark for the salvation of his household by which he condemned the world and

became an heir of the righteousness which is according to faith. (italics mine)

Same is true today, because the fire that will burn the earth is from above and is not visible. We only know it to be so because the Word of God tells us.

God uses foolish things to shame the wisdom of humanism. The present worldview is based on science and *objective* reality. To postmodernism, the metaphysical world is not real, or if it's real, it is unknowable. They still hold to the Kantian epistemology of separation between faith and reason. Reason and science are reality, while faith and God are unknown. This is present-day agnosticism.

Indeed, the building of an ark must have seemed foolish to many in Noah's day since there was no visible rain. The gospel must also appear foolish to many today, as they see no coming disaster and no objective proof of Christ. Faith, then, is foolishness. Yet as we read, just as it happened in Noah's day, it will also happen when Christ returns.

Interestingly, only a few were saved at the flood. Out of the population in Noah's day, only a few were left alive: eight souls. (1 Peter 3:20). Isaiah says, "Therefore the inhabitants of the earth are burned and few men left" (Isaiah 24:6). And Isaiah 13:12 says "I will make mortal man scarcer than pure gold, And mankind than the gold of Ophir."

Likewise, Jesus says, "Two women will be grinding at the mill; one will be taken and one will be left" (Matthew 24:41). Those left are the few men who are left at the end of this age. This is not the rapture, as some think. Those taken in Noah's day were taken away by the flood; those left were the survivors, which included only Noah and his family. It was the same as in the days of Lot. Only Lot and his two daughters escaped, a rather small number compared to the number of inhabitants in Sodom and Gomorrah. Those left at the end of the age will be few in comparison to the world's population. Those left were still in the flesh, and they, like Noah's family after the flood, were all that was left to populate the new earth. The body of Christ however will be changed into our new bodies and taken up.

You may say, "Yes, this is not the rapture because the church has already been taken at the beginning of the tribulation." But Jesus does mention the rapture. He says,

> But immediately after the tribulation of those days the sun will be darkened and the moon will not give its light, and the stars will fall from the sky and the power of the heavens will be shaken and then the sign of the Son of Man will appear in the sky and then all the tribes of the earth will mourn, and they will see the Son of Man coming on the clouds of the sky with power and great glory and he will send forth His angels with a great trumpet and they will gather together His elect from the four winds, from one end of the sky to the other. (Matthew 24:29–31)

Compare this to Paul's version in 2 Thessalonians 2:1: "Now we request you brethren with regard to the coming of our Lord Jesus Christ and our gathering together to Him." The coming and gathering are one and the same event, as Paul says, and this also agrees with what Christ says. Here is another example of Granville Sharp's rule for Greek grammar. Coming and gathering are the same event, and, therefore, they are at the same time—like the wheat is separated from the tares.

What is the significance of this for us, and why is it important to know some of these scriptural predictions? Indeed, if we already trust Christ as our Savior, then the Second Coming of Christ cannot change our outcome, for we are saved by faith not by having the end-time events figured out. But faith comes by hearing, and hearing comes by the Word of God. The message is to encourage our faith. Why go to church if you are already saved and cannot lose your salvation? To grow and continue in the faith. These are the accompaniments of faith. These are God's provisions for us so we can endure to the end. God's salvation includes the entire process. We still must persevere in the faith.

Now concerning the Second Coming, Jesus clearly states, "But of that day or hour no man knows, no not the angels of heaven, but My Father only" (Matthew 24:36 KJV). Therefore, whoever specifies the day or hour that the Lord will return is, by virtue of this verse, a false prophet because only the Father knows. Prophets who claim a spirit told them the day by vision cannot be believed either because angels are spirits, and Jesus said no angel knows. However, this verse has been taken out of context by many dispensationalists to preach a doctrine of imminency. Christ comes like a thief, so why study prophecy and look for signs because we do not know the day or hour? He does say, however, which watch of the night can be known. This means if you can count to seven, you may know the year.

Christ didn't say ignore the teaching about His coming, just because we don't know exactly when it may be. In fact, He suggests the very opposite: "Therefore be on the alert, for you do not know which day your Lord is coming" (Matthew 24:42). Since we do not know the day, we are commanded to be on the alert. He makes this same warning after the parable of the wise and foolish virgins.

We recall that the lamps of the foolish virgins went out at a critical time of night, when the bridegroom was coming. The foolish virgins then went off to buy oil and missed the bridegroom. The door was shut. We must continue in the faith until the very end. Jesus said, "If you abide in My word then you are truly disciples of Mine" (John 8:31).

The foolish virgins did not take oil with them in their flasks. "If anyone does not have the Spirit of Christ, he does not belong to Him" (Romans 8:9). The Spirit of Christ is evidence that we abide in the faith of Christ. Jesus said, "Abide in Me and I in you." The Holy Spirit abides in the believers (Galatians 3:14).

God wants us to be on the alert, like a watchman in the night, who, if His master comes, then he can open the door to Him immediately. Just as at the exodus, the people had to have their lamps burning and their garments on in readiness for departure and the blood on the lintel of their houses. This is what it means to be on the alert. Abiding in the faith. Believe in the name of His Son Jesus Christ and love one another. How do we believe? John 1:12 says "But as many as received Him, to those who believe in His name, He gave the right to become the children of God." Where meek souls will receive Him still the dear Christ enters in. (As at Bethlehem)

If your lamps are going out, or we are without a wedding garment, or you have not applied the blood of Christ to your heart, then we are not ready. We are still dead in our transgressions. The Greek word for *be alert* is γρηγορειτε, a form of the perfect tense of the verb "to be raised up" (present tense of εγειρω). With the perfect tense, it means to be in a state of being raised up. This is justification through faith. You still must receive Christ though to receive the forgiveness of your sins. Then the Holy Spirt will be poured out into your new heart. This is the New Covenant, a new heart and a new Spirit.

2

Olivet Discourse

Let's look again at the Olivet Discourse and see if there is a time line for these events. Although Christ said no one knows the day or the hour of His coming, we should not infer that we will be completely in the dark. Otherwise, what's the point of being on the alert? Watchfulness has to do with the Word of God. We must not be like the evil slave, who said in his heart, "My master is not coming for a long time," and begins to beat his fellow slaves and eat and drink with drunkards (Matthew 24:48–49). The evil slave is like the foolish virgins who fall away. This includes the slave who hid his Lords money.

I believe that Jesus gives us a time line in Matthew 24:37: "For the coming of the Son of Man will be just like the days of Noah." We discussed this earlier, but I would like us to see it in the context of the Olivet Discourse. The reference to the "the days of Noah" in the Greek, an article is placed in front, indicating an article of previous reference. Without an article, Jesus would be describing the kind of days such as evil days, but here, He is talking about a specific number of days. The specific days are mentioned in Genesis 7:4, where God says, "For *after* seven more days, I will send rain on the earth forty days and forty nights."

Then, in Genesis 7:10, Moses writes, "And it came about after the seven days that the water of the flood came upon the earth."

Then, in Genesis 7:13: "On the very same day Noah and Shem and Ham and Japheth the sons of Noah and Noah's wife and the three wives of his sons with them entered the ark." This was on the eighth day, after the seven days, just as God said.

On the same day that they entered the ark, the flood came—on the eighth day, after seven days. Jesus says that in the same way will the Son of Man come. These seven days, I believe, are equivalent to the seven years before Christ's Second Coming. Why might God give us this time line? Because man shall not live by bread alone but by every word that proceeds out of the mouth of God.

The entrance into the ark in Noah's day was the same as the entrance into the wedding feast: and those who were ready entered with him into the wedding feast (Matthew 25:10). When did the bridegroom and the five virgins enter the wedding feast? It must have been after the seven years, just like in the seven days of Noah. They did not lose faith but endured to the end. The foolish virgins took no oil and failed to enter. This is the prophesied apostasy.

Recall too that the Olivet Discourse continues until the end of Matthew 25. The context is key. The coming of the flood and Noah's entering the ark is compared to the coming of the Son of Man and our entering the wedding feast. The wedding feast is our entering into the kingdom of God when we receive our raptured bodies. Like in the days of Noah, Jesus creates a similar time line. In fact, the first event foreshadows the second. Jesus makes this comparison clear.

Throughout the book of Revelation is this repeating of sevens—the seven seals, the seven trumpets, the seven bowls, the forty-two months, half of seven, the times, time and a half, another half of seven. Noah and his family entered the ark after the seven days, on the eighth day, when the flood came. Jesus, by comparing His coming to Noah's flood, is giving us the same time line. It is after the seven-year tribulation period spoken of in Daniel 9:27 (the final week) that we expect Him to come. Yes, we would all prefer a pretribulation rapture, but this is God's salvation, not ours.

The final seven-year tribulation is discussed in Daniel 9:27. The prince who is to come will make a firm covenant with the many for one week but, in the middle of the week, will put a stop to the sacrifices and set up the abomination of desolation, referred to by Jesus in Matthew

24:15. The futurists are correct on this final week, and this is clearly seen in all the sevens in the book of Revelation.

Without this time line, many of the prophecies in Revelation seem to have no order. For example, the destruction of Babylon occurs in Revelation 18. After the judgment of Babylon, we have, in chapter 19, a great multitude in heaven, praising God for His judgments (19:1–6), followed by the marriage of the Lamb (19:7–10). These are definitely futuristic and refer to the tribulation period.

In Revelation 19:11–21, we have Christ's return on a white horse to judge the beast and his armies at Armageddon. This is at the end of the seven-year tribulation. But the rider on the white horse in Revelation 6:2 appears at the beginning of this final week. We must know the difference.

Compare this Armageddon to the war against Edom in Isaiah 34 and 63. *Edom* means red, and it may be the scarlet beast. It is at Armageddon that Christ pours out His wrath on the Antichrist and the false prophet and those who take the mark with fire and brimstone at His Second Coming. This is the wrath of God, preceded by the rapture. The wrath of God is to what Peter refers, in that the earth and its works are burned up.

It is important not to equate the tribulation period, which is Satan's wrath, where Babylon is destroyed (Revelation 18) to the wrath of God or Armageddon, where the Antichrist and his army are *destroyed by Christ* at His coming (2 Thessalonians 2:8; Revelation 19). The first occurs before the rapture; the latter, on the very day of but after the rapture. The wheat and the tares are harvested on the same day. This fits with Paul's account of the coming and gathering in 2 Thessalonians 2:1. And we should expect the same in the Olivet Discourse.

The judgment of Babylon with fire is done by the nations that joined up with the beast and the ten kings (Revelation 17:16; Isaiah 13:1–5). But the destruction of the scarlet beast and his army is done by Christ and His angels with fire at His advent (Isaiah 34; 63). This is Edom, which means red. This is the wrath of God. Armageddon includes God. The fall of Babylon is through the beast, the destroyer, the Antichrist. The beast turns on her and burns her with fire, even though she rides the beast at the start of tribulation.

The wrath of God is poured out on all who take the mark of the beast throughout the world (Revelation 14:9). These are the tares. They will be burned up, even as the beast and false prophet are thrown, alive, into the lake of fire and brimstone (Revelation 19:20). The inhabitants of the earth are burned, and few men are left.

Those who participate in the sins of Babylon by worshipping the beast and taking the mark of the beast will receive of her plagues. The call to God's people is to come out from the midst of her. There is a twofold warning here. Come out of religious Babylon to escape God's wrath, but also come out of commercial Babylon because in one hour, she will be burned with fire (Revelation 18:4). The false prophet escapes one but not the other. We will discuss the twofold Babylon in later chapters.

The warning by God to come out of Babylon is the same kind of warning for those in Judea to flee to the mountains when they see the abomination of desolation standing in the temple. These events take place during the tribulation, prior to the rapture, so it is necessary to leave because of war. Then, there will be tribulation such as has not been since the beginning of the world, nor ever shall be (Matthew 24:21).

Notice that Jesus says to those in Judea, only to flee into the mountains. But with Babylon, John, in Revelation 18:4, says, come forth from her midst. With Babylon, it is to be a complete destruction by fire, as when God overthrew Sodom and Gomorrah (Jeremiah 50:40; Revelation 18). But with Israel, there are captives, and they can survive by fleeing into the wilderness (Luke 21:21, 24). Isaiah 1:9 says, "Unless the Lord of hosts had left us a few survivors we would be like Sodom, we would be like Gomorrah." Not so with commercial Babylon—no survivors but those who leave before. No survivors from Sodom and Gomorrah, unless like Lot and his two daughters, you left.

Conversely, with Babylon, there is a call for a complete destruction with nothing left to her (Jeremiah 50:26). All there will be is the sound of fugitives and refugees fleeing from the land of Babylon (Jeremiah 50:28). She will be left like a wilderness, without inhabitant (Jeremiah 51:29). And it will be a perpetual desolation (Jeremiah 51:62). No one will ever inhabit Babylon again, forever (Jeremiah 50:39). Isaiah 13:20

says of Babylon, "It will never be inhabited or lived in from generation to generation." She will be like Sodom and Gomorrah. Not so with Israel.

The beginning of the tribulation, according to Revelation 6:1, is the opening of the first seal by Christ. This is the rider on a white horse (Revelation 6:2). This first seal corresponds with the sign of deception mentioned by Jesus in Matthew 24:4. Someone riding a white horse can easily be mistaken for Christ, as Christ does appear as such in Revelation 19. This rider in Revelation 6:2, however, is Antichrist, one saying, "I am Christ." This one comes to Israel, and this is when the final week of Daniel begins because the final week has to do with Israel.

The deception of Antichrist, which is someone saying "I am Christ," must include the apostasy as well, or the false teaching around him. Paul says,

> Let no man deceive you by any means: for that day shall not come, except there come a falling away first, and that man of sin be revealed, the son of perdition; Who opposes and exalts himself above all that is called God, or that is worshipped; so that he as God sits in the temple of God, shewing himself that he is God. (2 Thessalonians 2:3–4 KJV)

This is Antichrist, the many saying, "I am Christ," just as Paul mentions. Greek scholars certainly know that the Greek word for the temple, mentioned here by Paul, is ναος and does not refer to the Jewish physical temple but the church of God. The Greek word for the physical temple is ιερον, used twenty-five times in the book of Acts. Not once does Luke in Acts use ναος. Therefore, when Paul says in 2 Thessalonians that Antichrist sits in the temple of God, he is speaking of the church, not the Jewish temple, which doesn't even exist.

According to Paul, the Antichrist is already seated in the church, and his deception is in the church as well. Paul and Jesus warn about deception, not to those poor unfortunate souls who will not be raptured but to the present church of God. Satan deceived Eve in paradise. This warning is for us so that we, as God's people, might awake to the approaching thief who comes to kill, steal, and destroy. Persecution is the fifth seal in Revelation 6.

When Jesus was praying in the garden of Gethsemane while the disciples slept, it was because Judas was coming. Only Jesus was ready; the rest fled. Antichrist is coming, but the true church will be warned and will be ready.

> Children it is the last hour and just as you heard that antichrist is coming even now many antichrists have arisen from this, we know that it is the last hour. (1 John 2:18)

John is warning the church about the coming Antichrist. The deception is no warning, or we just don't know. This is part of the deception concerning Antichrist that Jesus says will be evident as we draw near to the last hour.

The second sign that Jesus mentions is, "and you will be hearing of wars and rumors of war see that you be not troubled" (Matthew 24:6). The second seal in Revelation 6:4 is the red horse of war. The third sign Jesus mentions is famine, and this corresponds with the black horse of Revelation 6:5.

Finally, in the textus receptus of Matthew 24:7, it reads και λοιμοι "and pestilence." Here, pestilence means any deadly infectious malady (Vine 1984, 470). This is the pale horse in Revelation 6:7, and together, these represent the four horsemen of the Apocalypse. This is like COVID-19, but the order is wrong, and so we are not yet in the final week. However, it gives us a glimpse of what the pale horse will entail and certainly gives us warning of the nearness of the final seven-year tribulation period. Whose is to say this virus will not just mutate and carry on? Britain is just now experiencing this.

After the first four seals and signs in Matthew 24, Jesus says, "But all these are merely the beginning of birth pangs" (Matthew 24:8). This term birth pangs in the Greek is ωδινων, the plural form of the singular ωδιν. These four horsemen are only the "birth pangs, "or beginning, of sorrows, as the King James Version uses "sorrows" for birth pangs. But *birth pangs* is a key Greek word here because the word appears in

Revelation 12:2 with regard to the woman clothed with the sun and the moon under her feet: "And she was with child, and she cried out being in labor and in pain to give birth." John uses the present participle feminine form of the verb ωδινω, ωδινουσα. This woman was having birth pangs, just like the birth pangs that Jesus mentioned in Matthew 24:8. The fact that John uses the same word in Revelation 12:2 as Jesus uses at the beginning of the tribulation places each event in the same time slot.

This must be the first half of the tribulation because later in Revelation 12:14, the woman flees into the wilderness, away from the presence of the dragon for "a time, times, and half a time," or three and one-half years. This is the church of Christ in the tribulation. Mount Zion, a city set on a hill. (Matt. 5:14b). The city of God, the holy dwelling places of the Most High. (Psalm 46:6). "Do you not know that you are a temple of God and the Spirit of God dwells in you?" (1 Cor. 3:16).

The next thing Jesus says is, "Then they will deliver you up to tribulation, and will kill you, and you will be hated by all nations on account of My name" (Matthew 24:9). This parallels with what happened to the woman in Revelation 12:13—"And when the dragon saw that he was thrown down to the earth, he persecuted the woman who gave birth to the male child." Persecution is the fifth seal, according to Revelation 6:9, and this follows exactly the order of events mentioned in Matthew 24:4–10.

Satan, then, is the persecutor in the birth-pangs stage, or the first half of the final week, but this changes both in Revelation 13, with the rise of Antichrist, the beast of the sea, and when the abomination of desolation is set up in Matthew 24:15. The last half of the tribulation is the work of Antichrist after he is indwelt by Satan who is cast out of heaven. The pandemic is Satan's persecution then just the birth-pangs.

3

Historical View of Revelation

As we study Revelation, we must not just focus on the future seven years that we miss the things that are now historical. The futurist and preterist view of the book of Revelation overlooks the historical view of what already has happened and is now history. The futurists and preterists take the focus off what the Reformers said about the beast of Revelation 13:1 and place it at some future or past date. They are waiting for an Antichrist who will help build the temple of God in Jerusalem and then take his seat in it, as 2 Thessalonians 2:4 *seems* to say. Unfortunately, this is not what 2 Thessalonians 2:4 is talking about. Neither did Nero fulfill 2 Thessalonians 2:4.

This will be discussed in more detail later, but for now, as mentioned, the Greek word for temple in 2 Thessalonians 2:4 is not used for the physical Jewish temple but for the church of God. The Greek word for temple in 2 Thessalonians 2:4 is ναος, not ιερον, the word for the Jewish temple. According to the historical view of Revelation, the Antichrist is already sitting in the church of God, showing himself to be God. The beast from the sea in Revelation 13:1 is the little horn from Daniel 7:8.

Now according to the image of Daniel and the book of Revelation the order is the dragon, imperial Rome, the beast from the sea, Papal Rome or the Holy Roman Empire. These are the two legs of iron. They are identical with seven heads and ten horns. The beast is both a kingdom and a king.

The papacy ran uninterrupted from the 8th century when they gained papal lands until 1798 when the temporal powers were taken away. The

Holy Roman Empire also ceased at this time when Napoleon defeated the last emperor Francis II. This is the end of the iron legs of Rome, the sixth head. This is followed historically by the beast of the earth. Then in Revelation 17:1-3 just before the judgment on the woman who rides the scarlet beast, we have the iron and clay of the image. Chapter 17 is the eight head, the beast revived from the deadly wound. This is the iron in the feet. The feet is futuristic and is forming before our eyes. Reformers interpreted this merely historically also an error.

The futurists believe that the book of Revelation is all future and will be fulfilled in the seventieth week of Daniel, before which the church will be raptured. The beast would be the new Babylon, a modern-day world system headed up by the Antichrist. He will be a charismatic world leader who unites all nations, and he will make war with the Jews and build their temple. This is true but the historical is important for us to understand what we have before us. Just like the image of Daniel helps us understand Revelation.

The futurist view of Antichrist quotes Matthew 24:15 and has Antichrist "standing" in the holy place, while the historical Antichrist, according to 2 Thessalonians 2:4, has him seated in the temple of the church. According to the historical view, the pope is the little horn, the beast, and is now seated in the place of Christ in the church. Futurists say that the little horn is not the pope but some future leader. This future world leader will head up the new Babylon, a world empire with one money. Futurists misidentified the antichrist and the historicists misidentified Babylon.

Futurism, contrary to popular belief, did not begin with Protestantism. On the contrary, the futurist interpretation of the book of Revelation was a counteraction by Rome to the Reformers' claim of the pope as Antichrist. The Reformers identified the papacy with the little horn of Daniel and the beast of Revelation 13. They also identified the Roman Catholic Church with the whore of Babylon in Revelation 17. Here we may lean towards the futurism since Revelation 17 is seen in John as just before the judgment of the woman Babylon. Her judgment is in Revelation 18 hardly the Roman Catholic Church. The Reformers presumed the beast to be the Pope and the woman to be the church of Rome. Yet as we suggested by the feet of iron and clay the woman is really America, the beast from the land. America had not yet appeared on the scene.

The historical view of Revelation was countered by several Jesuit works, beginning in 1591, by Francisco Ribera and, later, Manuel Lacunza (1731–1801). These two adopted a futurist view of Revelation. The futurists said the book of Revelation is all future, and the beast who blasphemes God for forty-two months is a future Antichrist who will take his seat in a rebuilt Jewish temple at the end. This later evolved into dispensationalism under John Nelson Darby and others in the 1830s. Attached to dispensationalism is the pretribulation rapture.

The futurists then countered the Reformation claim of the pope as Antichrist and the Roman Catholic Church as Babylon. John kind of blends religious Babylon with kingdom Babylon. We see this in 2 Thessalonians 2:7 where Paul says the mystery of iniquity is already at work. Religious Babylon is there in false religion but will not be revealed until the man of sin is revealed. The Popes carry this apostate Christianity. Through Rome then comes the persecutions of religious Babylon.

The fifth seal of Revelation 6 has the souls of these martyrs crying out to God for their blood to be avenged or judged. This too was placed into the future. The Reformers said the martyrs were descriptive of the woman Babylon, who is drunk with the blood of the martyrs and the witnesses of Jesus—not future but history. This denial of the historical view of the Reformers is prevalent today among Evangelicals. We cannot deny the persecutions of the Roman system throughout the middle ages.

I believe in the historical view of Revelation but also in the future view. They are both evident. These can be reconciled. Babylon also has a future aspect as commercial Babylon, seen in Revelation 18, where Babylon is depicted as a wealthy commercial system to be destroyed in one day by fire. This cannot be equated with the Roman Catholic Church or the Vatican, which was built on 109 acres and is certainly not a commercial power like the Babylon over which *all the merchants of the earth mourn* when she is destroyed. For the judgment of the woman in Revelation 17 is recorded in 18. Same woman.

The mystery of iniquity was already at work in Paul's day (2 Thessalonians 2:7). This is the apostate religion. The coming judgment of mystery Babylon was announced in Revelation 17:1 and mentioned again in Revelation 18. This must be just before the stone comes and strikes the image on the feet of iron and clay. This is the daughter of Babylon, the woman riding the beast.

Personally, I believe the woman riding the scarlet beast represent the feet of iron and clay. The clay is just the beast from the earth and the iron the beast from the sea. America rides the beast. A New Babylon, a New World Order? Both are Babylon as the two have become one flesh.

These seem to be the two beasts of Revelation 13 merging in the feet of iron and clay. Now this is not what the Reformers believed for they made Babylon the Roman Catholic Church. The problem is that this woman was sitting on seven mountains when John wrote Revelation. No Roman Catholic Church in AD 95. But neither was there an America. For now lets hear the historical view.

Now we will focus on the first beast and the woman who rides him. Mystery Babylon is drunk with the blood of the saints. This historically is seen in the persecutions of pagan Rome by the Caesars and papal Rome by the Roman Catholic Church, during and before the Reformation. Her work is not complete, according to the historical view, but there is a futurism then.

The souls of these martyrs must wait until the rest of their brethren are killed in the same way as them—by the same persecuting power that killed some fifty million Christians from 1200 until 1800 (Foxe's Book of Martyrs 2001). Futurism wants to deny this fact and put all into the last seven years. Sorry, but if we do not learn from history, then we are destined to repeat it.

When does this second phase of persecutions take place? During the tribulation. We do not deny the futuristic aspect of the tribulation, but my point is that we must not forget the historical view of Revelation either. The witness of the inquisition and Reformers is with blood and is a historical fact. No one can deny what Romanism has done. But this is just what the little horn or the beast will do as he makes ware with the saints. This is still the beast of the sea and the second leg of iron. But whether it is pagan worship or papal worship both seem to be mystery Babylon. Satan is the father of this religion.

Even as Polycarp and many of the early Christians were martyred because they refused to worship Caesar, even so the Reformers were burned as heretics because they denounced the pope as the Antichrist. The same persecution will be in the tribulation for those who denounce the Antichrist and refuse to worship him, his image or take his mark. This must be Popery and Romanism.

The futurist view was a counter-Reformation and has its roots in Romanism. The purpose of the Jesuits was to hide the truth of the Reformation, which declared the papacy as the Antichrist (Wikipedia, "Francisco Ribera"). Thus came forth futurism, partly true but also denying the elephant in the room.

In the late Middle Ages and in the wake of the Protestant Reformation, accusations of being the Antichrist were leveled against the popes. Amid the controversy, Ribera, in 1585, began writing a lengthy (five-hundred-page) commentary on the book of Revelation, titled *In Sacrum Beati Ioannis Apostoli, & Evangelistiae Apocalypsin Commentarii*, proposing that the first chapters of the apocalypse applied to ancient pagan Rome, and the rest referred to a yet future period of three and a half literal years, immediately prior to the Second Coming (Wikipedia, "Francisco Ribera").

This futurist view was taken up by Protestants, such as John Nelson Darby, a clergyman born in England but who served in Ireland. John Nelson Darby (November 18, 1800–April 29, 1882) was an Anglo-Irish Bible teacher, one of the influential figures among the original Plymouth Brethren, and the founder of the Exclusive Brethren. He is considered to be the father of modern dispensationalism and futurism.

Pretribulation rapture theology was popularized extensively in the 1830s by John Nelson Darby and the Plymouth Brethren and further popularized in the United States in the early twentieth century by the wide circulation of the Scofield Reference Bible. (Wikipedia, "John Nelson Darby").

While this teaching has some good points, in that it recognizes a seven-year tribulation, it served the purpose of its originators, namely to muddy the waters in the interpretation of the book of Revelation so as to take the focus off the papacy. However, it was not the book of Revelation that identified the pope as antichrist but Paul's prophecy of Antichrist in 2 Thessalonians 2:4.

Wayne Grant

Concerning the beast and the woman who rides him in Revelation 17, it seems better to side with futurism. Daniel has the mixing of the iron and the clay in the feet of the image. This is interpreted I believe by John as the woman riding the scarlet beast. This event takes place in Revelation 17 just before her judgment. That judgment is Revelation 18, followed by Christ's return in Revelation 19. Therefore, I take this woman to be America the land beast joined up with antichrist the sea beast. The beast from the sea which we said was Papal Rome does not have a woman riding it. But in Revelation 17:3 the woman rides the beast. Therefore, the woman riding the scarlet beast is future and not during the middle ages. The legs of iron are the dragon and the Holy Roman Empire. Each lasting about 1000 years. Imperial Rome ending in AD 476 is not the deadly wound simply because the wound is on *one of the heads of the beast* not the dragon. Therefore, it is better to take the deadly wound with what happened in 1805 when the Holy Roman Empire ended and the Pope was removed from Rome and died in exile and his temporal power was ended in 1798. This is the final leg in Daniels image. Following this comes the beast from the earth.

This beast arises in the earth as opposed to the sea, which is referred in Revelation to tongues and nations and peoples. North America was an uninhabited area. Now America becomes the seventh head which would arise after the sixth head had ended. But the sixth head is only wounded but is healed in 1814 with the return of the popes to Rome. The pope is the head of the beast and they begin the new European Union which is the kingdom of the beast. This is the feet. Now just as the Papal Rome was only iron in the image it must be the iron in the feet of the image. The woman must be the clay which units with the scarlet beast. Here is where we need wisdom. The woman sits on seven mountains. But these are still part of the seven heads of the scarlet beast.

This is America who heads up the seven heads and the beast/antichrist who heads up the ten horns. These two beasts are the beast from the sea and the land beast shown by John in the composite picture of a woman riding a beast. This whole image falls at the same time. This entire union is Babylon and must include apostate Christianity.

In 2 Thessalonians 2:4, we have the religious side of the Antichrist, "who opposes and exalts himself above every so-called God or object of

22

worship so that he sits in the temple of God showing himself to be God." This is the Antichrist, beginning as the bishop of Rome and exalting himself to the claims of being Holy Father; vicar of Christ; the head of the church; infallible; the way, the truth, and the life, etc. First John 2:22 says, "Who is the liar but the one who denies that Jesus is the Christ? This is the antichrist the one who denies the Father and the Son." The pope denies the Father by calling himself Holy Father, and he denies that Jesus is *the Christ* by claiming to be another Christ. That is what "vicar of Christ" means—another Christ, *Vicarius Christi*. On his triple-crown tiara are the words *Vicarius Filii Dei*, which means, in Latin, "representative of the Son of God." If you add up the letters in Latin, you get 666. If he is not the Antichrist, then he is most unfortunate in perfectly fitting the description. (Spurgeon)

This event may be spoken of in Jesus's account in Matthew 12:25: "Any kingdom divided against itself is laid waste and any city or house divided against itself shall not stand. And if Satan casts out Satan, he is divided against himself how then shall his kingdom stand?" (Matthew 12:25) This is when the entire statue in Daniel 2 falls as a composite when the stone strikes its feet. The entire statue will fall. This is Satan's end time kingdom, the feet of iron and clay. This is the second fall of Babylon at the second coming of Christ. The scarlet beast along with those united with him.

Presently, the crown is on the seventh head, which I believe is America, the last world empire before the end. This is the old Babylonian/Assyrian Empire, seen in the seven heads and ten horns. This new world order some see as the G7, headed by America, united with the ten horns of the European Union. This is the woman riding the beast. These are the beast from the sea and the beast from the earth. Assyria is associated with the king of the north and Antichrist. Babylon, here, is commercial Babylon, the woman in the ephah who is carried to the land of Shinar and set there on her pedestal—America the great.

This text in Matthew 12:25 mentioned above needs to be coupled with Matthew 12:43:

Now when the unclean spirit goes out of a man it passes through waterless places seeking rest and does not find it. Then it says I will return to my house from which I came and when it comes it finds it unoccupied swept and put in order. Then it goes and takes along with it seven other spirits more wicked than itself and they go in and live there and the last state of that man becomes worse than the first.

This is the apostasy. Now Babylon is this house which has become a dwelling place of demons and a prison of every unclean spirit and a prison of every unclean and hateful bird." (Rev. 18:2). Paul says that day will not come unless the apostasy comes first and the man of lawlessness is revealed. (2 Thess. 2:3). The unclean spirit who takes along with himself seven other spirits is the eighth beast or antichrist.

Having had the deadly wound he comes out of the abyss and returns to the house from which he left. This *COULD BE* when the pope comes to America. He has returned to the house from which he was cast out.

Now in 1865 the US cast out the popes because they were accused of plotting the death of Lincoln after the south lost the war. However, on January 10, 1984 the United States formally recognized the Holy See when Ronald Reagan and Pope John Paul II agreed to establish diplomatic relations.

This *COULD BE* when the unclean spirit returns to the house. from which he was cast out. The establishment of diplomatic relations has opened the door to this union between the beast and the woman Babylon. We may be witnessing this very union between America and the Vatican. The last state of the man is then worse than the first is also used of the apostasy in 2 Peter 2:20. Here is the woman riding the beast, when the iron and the clay unite to form the final Satanic kingdom before the second coming of Christ. The apostasy must come first. Receiving a different gospel.

Now the beast needs the woman America to accomplish world government. This may be the new world order.

The lamb-like beast does not have ten horns on its head, like the dragon or the beast of the sea, but only two. Therefore, it is a different head, and it must be separate from Rome, even as America is a different head. She too is divided even as the two feet in the image. America is divided today. Rome cannot be the seventh head because this head remains for a short time and Rome lasted 2000 years in its two legs. But America is only 250 years. She is the clay, the land beast with two horns, divided and destined to fall. Fallen fallen, is Babylon the great, both the iron and the clay. Every divided kingdom will not stand Jesus says.

Only a nation coming up late in history can fulfill the seventh-head symbolism. To continue for a short time and be the last makes it an end-time empire, the last one. And since the beast of the earth is the last beast mentioned, it must be the seventh head of the dragon. This is the woman Babylon. The beast that was and is not and yet is must be the scarlet beast with the woman riding it. These two are the iron and the clay. They are the seventh and the eighth head combined in the feet. The two beasts of Revelation 13.

This woman is also called the daughter of Babylon, the commercial Babylon in Revelation 18, the woman in the ephah (a commercial symbol) set up in the land of Shinar, mentioned in Zechariah 5:7 (Gaebelein, 1911). America is the only present-day world power that can boast of the riches and mercantile traffic expressed in Revelation 18. She is Babylon too!

> Your mother shall be sore confounded; she that bare you
> shall be ashamed; behold the hindermost of the nations
> *shall be* a wilderness, a dry land and a desert. (Jeremiah
> 50:12 KJV)

Hindermost means last. The seventh is the last. See also, Jeremiah 50–51 on the daughter of Babylon. We will discuss this later.

4

Reformer's View of Rome

What Luther describes in the Reformation is the first fall of religious Babylon. But political Rome, as the fourth beast of Daniel, continued, even to the feet and toes of the image in Daniel 2:44, which is destroyed at the Second Coming, when the stone strikes the image on the feet. However, like the image of Dagon, religious Babylon had a fall during the Reformation, but the idol was set up again. Even today, the papacy is alive and well, with no one suspecting the pope as the Antichrist or little horn of Daniel 7. There must be a final fall of Babylon, when the entire image of Daniel 2 comes crashing down and when Dagon is broken. The beast still has ten horns—the future European Union one hour with the beast.

The first fall, then, is described by Luther as the work of the Spirit during the Reformation, speaking the Word of God to consume the man of sin.

> And then that lawless one will be revealed whom the Lord will consume with *the breath of His mouth* and bring to an end by the appearance of His coming. (2 Thessalonians 2:8 italics mine)

This is a twofold judgment on religious Babylon, which, like the image of Dagon, is broken at the second fall. As Christ is the image of the invisible God, so Antichrist is the visible image of Satan. Like the image of Dagon, it is a false god. We must expose this idol for what it is.

This was Luther's belief. He believed God would use us to contend for the faith and that this would be how Antichrist would be consumed at the end, broken by Christ Himself.

To those who think it's unnecessary for us to contend for the faith or that the gospel is not the sword of the Spirit, I refer you to Galatians 1:6–9: "I marvel that ye are so soon removed from him that called you into the grace of Christ unto another gospel." (The Greek ετερος is the word for "another of a different kind.") Then, Galatians 1:7—"which is not another; but there be some that trouble you and would pervert the gospel of Christ." (The Greek αλλος "another" of the same kind.) But though we or an angel from heaven preaches any other gospel unto you than that which we have preached unto you, let him be accursed. Here, the apostle does a play on the word another, switching from ετερος to αλλος and back to ετερος. Αλλος is another of the same kind. The gospel the Judaizers were preaching to the Galatians was not the same kind as the gospel of Paul; it is a different gospel, not the faith but a perversion of it. Paul calls this another law, the law of sin and death.

Likewise, the present ecumenical agreement on justification from October 31, 1999, is still a perversion of justification by faith alone. It is the law of sin and death. The same tree of the knowledge of good and evil that the serpent tempted Eve with. Paul says clearly that we are justified by faith apart from works. This is the true gospel, the tree of life. But they say that justification is unto good works. They argue that faith without works is dead, and so justification cannot be by faith alone. But Paul says what is not of faith is sin. He is the man of sin because he denies faith alone. This is a misunderstanding of James. Faith works through love, Paul says (Galatians 5:6.) But Roman Catholics say, "If the faith that justifies us be that which works by love, then faith alone does not justify." To the doctrine of faith alone, the popes have said anathema.

But Paul says anathema to those who preach a different gospel. What James is talking about is true faith. True faith has works. Faith bears fruit, just as every branch that does not bear fruit is cast off. Every branch that does not bear fruit is cut off and dries up and is burned for firewood.

Luther said,

Justification pertains to man, and not to works; for man is either justified and saved, or judged and condemned, and not works. Neither is it a controversy among the godly, that man is not justified by works, but righteousness must come from some other source than from his own works; for Moses, writing of Abel, says "The Lord had respect unto Abel, and to his offering." First, He had respect to Abel himself, then to his offering; because Abel was first counted righteous and acceptable to God, and then for his sake his offering was accepted also, and not he because of his offering. Again, God had no respect to Cain, and therefore neither to his offering: therefore, you see that regard is first to the worker, then to the work." (Wiersbe 1977, 346)

Justification is our death to sin. He who has died is justified from sin. Without this, we are still in our sins. Justification is really the gospel. Concerning those who deny justification, Luther says,

Whereby one becomes a Carthusian monk, another chooses some other order of monks, and another is consecrated a priest; some torment their flesh by wearing hair-cloth, others scourge their bodies with whips, others afflict themselves in a different manner; but these are of Cain's progeny, and their works are no better than his; for they continue the same that they were before, ungodly, and without justification; there is a change made of outward works only, of apparel, of place, etc. (Luther ad loc, 348)

For Evangelicals to join up with this ecumenical movement is to give support for *another* gospel. Why not put in their statement of faith what the Westminster Confession says?

VI. There is no other head of the Church, but the Lord Jesus Christ;(n) nor can the Pope of Rome, in any

> sense, be head thereof; but is that Antichrist, that man of sin, and son of perdition, that exalteth himself, in the Church, against Christ and all that is called God. (Westminster Confession, 1646, ch.25, VI)

But the new confession of the ecumenical movement is one under the headship of the Roman pontiff. This is a denial of Jesus Christ as the head of the church. Antichrist takes the place of Christ.

When we join with this apostasy, we participate in the sins of Babylon and, therefore, will reap her plagues. We are to come out of Babylon, not go into her. You have been severed from Christ, you who are seeking to be justified by law (Galatians 5:4). Justification by works is a false gospel.

This is part of Rome's counter-Reformation, to take back what was lost in the Reformation; to set up the false god again. But once again, the gospel shall cause her to fall, just as it did with Luther, Knox, Wycliffe, Tyndale, Calvin, Thomas Cranmer, Hus, and many others, who, before and after them, preached it. What fellowship has light with darkness … or what agreement has the temple of God with idols? (2 Corinthians 6:16).

5

Rapture According to 1 Thessalonians 4:13–17

Let us return to the subject of the rapture. This is spoke of in 1 Thessalonians 4:13–18 by the apostle Paul.

In verse 13, Paul writes, "But we do not want you to be uninformed brethren about those who are asleep that you may not grieve as do the rest who have no hope". When Paul begins a new subject, he often uses the Greek particle δε here, translated as *but*. He does not want his brethren to be "not knowing" concerning those who are sleeping. This participle "those who are sleeping" refers to Christians who have already died and have gone to be with the Lord. For these, we ought not to grieve because we are not without hope, like the rest.

With Greek participles, the *kind of action* is more important than the time of the action. Here, the focus is on the *kind of action*, and since this is a present tense, the focus is on *continuous action*—"those who are sleeping." Paul is saying that those who have died in Christ are asleep, not dead. It refers to those who have died but are still alive spiritually, but since they do not yet have their new bodies, they are in a state of rest. We must be true to the text.

Paul, here, is making a refutation of an early form of amillennialism. Amillennialism does not, as some think, simply mean *no millennium*. What it says is that the millennial reign of Christ began after His ascension. They think the thousand years is only spiritual and means the church age.

According to this view, all those who died in Christ are now reigning with Christ in the church age, which is the millennial reign of Christ. This is refuted by Paul, when he says the dead in Christ are asleep, not reigning yet. Roman Catholicism has held to a form of this view through its belief in the intercession of the prayers of the dead saints, such as Mary and the apostles. Unfortunately, they have failed to read 1 Thessalonians 4:13 and try to comfort people with an unscriptural teaching; namely, that Christians are reigning right now with Christ in the millennium. This is amillennialism.

We are premillennialists. We believe the scriptures teach that Christ returns at the beginning of the millennium to raise the dead in Christ. Another teaching, which is the extreme in the other direction, is to believe in annihilation, where the soul, body, and spirit of men cease to exist until the resurrection. This view is sometimes called *soul sleep*. Jesus brings with Him those who have fallen asleep in Christ. Where are the dead in Christ? In paradise. Jesus said to the thief, today you will be with Me in paradise. Paradise is heaven. (See 2 Corinthians 12:2–4.) Absent from the body is present with the Lord (2 Corinthians 5:8).

Some seek to alter the text in Luke 23:43 in order to support their doctrine of soul sleep. Jesus said to the thief on the cross, "Truly I say to you, today you will be with Me in paradise" (Luke 23:43). According to some, this should read, "Truly I say to you today, you will be with Me in paradise." Consequently, this promise of paradise becomes some future promise of who knows when. But in the Greek text—all the Greek references are from the fourth revised edition of the *Greek New Testament*—it reads, Αμην σοι λεγω, σημερον μετ' εμου εση εν τω παραδεισω (Aland 1983). The comma is placed before *today*, just like the Bible translators say. The spirit of this man would go to be with the Lord, not annihilation.

As mentioned, the annihilation view claims that the body, soul, and spirit all cease to exist at death. This is in contradiction to what Jesus said to the thief. The thief, after his death and before the sun went down, would be with Jesus in heaven. If that is not eternal life, then I don't know what is. Paradise lost is now paradise restored in Christ.

Paul uses the same words in Philippians 1:23–24:

> But I am hard-pressed from both directions, having the desire to depart and be with Christ, for that is very much better; yet to remain on in the flesh is more necessary for your sake.

To depart *and be with Christ* is the same as Jesus's statement, "Today you will *be with Me* in Paradise." Paul says this would be very much better. This would not be so if death was annihilation.

In the story of the rich man and Lazarus, after Lazarus died, he was taken away by the angels to Abraham's bosom, a Jewish equivalent of paradise. (See Josephus 1987, 813) The rich man, however, dies and wakes up in Hades. This clearly teaches life after death, either in paradise or in Hades. How can we say the soul of the rich man is asleep?

Next, in 1 Thessalonians 4:14, Paul says, "For if we believe that Jesus died and rose again. Even so God will bring with Him those who have fallen asleep in Jesus." The particle *for* implies reason, and the reason we do not grieve like the rest, who have no hope, is because we believe Jesus died and rose again and that God will bring with Him those who have fallen asleep in Jesus. *Fallen asleep* simply means they have died in the flesh. Their spirits are with Christ. When Christ returns, He will bring with Him the spirits of those who have fallen asleep in Christ, in order to be united with their new bodies.

Next, Paul says, "For this we say to you by the word of the Lord, that we who are alive and remain until the coming of the Lord shall not precede those who have fallen asleep" (1 Thessalonians 4:15). This is according to the word of the Lord, Paul says.

We who are alive and remain until the Second Coming of Christ will not precede those who have fallen asleep. Here, we have the order of the resurrection. This order is also stated in 1 Corinthians 15:23: "But each in his own order; Christ the first fruits, after that those who are Christ's at His coming." Those include not only the living but also the dead in Christ.

Next, Paul says, "For the Lord Himself will descend from heaven with a shout, with the voice of an archangel, and with the trumpet of

God; and the dead in Christ shall rise first" (1 Thessalonians 4:16). This is exactly what Jesus says in John 11:26—notice the order: "I am the resurrection and the life." The dead in Christ rise first; then, those alive will be changed, and together they are caught up to meet the Lord.

Paul explains how this will happen. The Lord Himself will descend from heaven. This is the sign of the Son of Man in heaven. And Matthew 24:30 says, "And they will see the Son of Man coming on the clouds of heaven with power and great glory." This is the descent of Christ from heaven, the sign the apostles asked of His coming and the end of the age (Matthew 24:3). Christ comes with great power and glory, most visible. Glory is great light, like lightning shining from one end of the sky to the other. Great power—this is the rolling back of the heavens, like a scroll, like the tearing of the veil and a sudden, great infusion of light. His light lit up the whole world (Psalm 97:4). Makes no difference if it is day or night.

Why does Paul emphasize that we are caught up in the air? The reason is that the tares and the wheat are separated at the same time. He is going to burn up his adversaries, the tares, and we are raptured out and, like the wheat, are gathered into barns. On the very same day that Noah entered the ark, the flood came and took them all away. On the very same day that Lot left Sodom and Gomorrah, fire and brimstone rained down from heaven. On the same day that the tares were burned up, the wheat was gathered into barns. This is the rapture, in order to escape the wrath of God. This is different with Babylon.

With Babylon, He says, Come out of her, my people (Revelation 18:4). This command is something we have to do in order to escape her coming judgment (Revelation 18). The angels are not involved because the harvest has not yet come. This is only the tribulation. The fall of Babylon then must precede the rapture. Jesus says,

> But immediately *after* the tribulation of those days the
> sun will be darkened and the moon will not give its light
> and the stars will fall from heaven and the powers of the
> heavens will be shaken. (Matthew 24:29)

Then does the sign of the Son of Man appear in heaven, the sign of the end of the age. But this sign is *after* the tribulation. Babylon falls during the tribulation! The church, then, must come out of Babylon before she is destroyed by fire, contrary to popular belief.

I would like to look at an important phrase that Paul uses in 1 Thessalonians 4:17. The phrase is "to meet" the Lord in the air. The word in the Greek is απαντησιν. "It seems that the special idea of the word was the official welcome of a newly arrived dignitary" (Moulton, 2009, 53)

This is the same Greek word used for the ten virgins in Matthew 25:6: "But at midnight there was a shout, Behold the bridegroom! Come out *to meet* Him". Paul says *we will meet* Him in the air, referring to the rapture.

Also, Matthew 25:1 says, "Then the kingdom of heaven will be comparable to ten virgins who took their lamps and went out *to meet* the bridegroom". Here is another form of the same word. We know that only the wise actually met the Lord; the foolish went away to buy oil. Paul says, "We who are alive and remain will be caught up together with them in the clouds to meet the Lord in the air." (1 Thessalonians 4:17)

The point is that Paul is using a word for *rapture* that also occurs in Matthew 25:1, 6, in the context of the coming of the bridegroom. This is no coincidence. These scriptures talk about the same events. Paul says, "For this cause a man shall leave his father and mother and shall cleave to his wife and the *two shall become one flesh*" (Ephesians 5:31–32 italics mine).

The marriage is when the two become one flesh. This is exactly what happens when we are raptured; we are changed. We will have the same new body as Christ. Revelation 19:7 places this marriage of the Lamb *after* the fall of Babylon but before the white-horse judgment (Revelation 19:11).

Colossians 3:3,4 says, "For you have died and your life is hidden with Christ in God. When Christ, who is our life is revealed, then you also will be revealed with Him in glory." The rapture comes when Christ is revealed from heaven.

6

Antichrist Revealed in the Church

Another important end-of-the-age passage is 2 Thessalonians 2. Paul begins by saying, "Now we request you brethren with regard to the coming of our Lord Jesus Christ and our gathering together to Him" (2 Thessalonians 2:1). This verse follows the same Greek construction used by the apostle Matthew in Matthew 24:3: "And what will be the sign of Your coming and end of the age?" Both these passages place two events under one article. As I've mentioned, this is called Granville Sharpe's rule for Greek grammar. The two events are one and the same event. The coming and gathering in 2 Thessalonians 2:1 are at the same time. The sign of "Your coming" and "end of the age" are on the same day.

Paul, then, right at the beginning of 2 Thessalonians 2, is teaching the Thessalonian church an important fact; namely, that the Second Coming of Christ and our gathering are not separate events. The Greek word for *gathering* is the same word for the angels gathering the wheat into His barn (Matthew 13:30). The word in the Greek is συναγαγετε in Matthew 13:30 and means "to gather together." In Matthew 24:31, the same word is used but has the added preposition, επι (επισυωαξουσιν).

In both passages in Matthew, the angels gather together the elect, or the wheat. In 2 Thessalonians 2:1, Paul uses the noun form of this word (επισυωαγωγης) and refers to our gathering. According to *Vine's Expository Dictionary* (1984), the preposition epi (= to) is used with "to gather together," suggesting stress upon the place at which the gathering is made, like a hen gathering her chicks under her wings (261). It is therefore quite plain that Paul equates our gathering to the rapture, and he is taking Jesus's own words in describing this gathering.

Next, Paul says, "We request you brethren … that you may not be quickly shaken from your composure or disturbed either by a spirit or a message or a letter as if from us, to the effect that the day of the Lord has come" (2 Thessalonians 2:2). The Greek word for "to be disturbed" is the infinitive θροεισθαι. This is the same word used in Matthew 24:6—"see that you are not frightened"; ορατε μη θροεισθε. Paul deliberately takes words from Jesus's own account of early signs in the Olivet Discourse.

Paul says not to be frightened or shaken, either by some charismatic spirit or letter or message from us, to the effect that the day of the Lord has come. The words *has come*, or has arrived, is perfect tense and means completed action with continuous results, with emphasis on the *continuous results*. Someone had told them that the day of the Lord already had happened. When wars and rumors of wars or pestilence or famine come, we are not to be frightened (Matthew 24:6). We are not to panic when these signs start happening. Paul is saying, do not listen to these false prophets, no matter what they say because two things must precede the day of the Lord; the apostasy and the revelation of the man of sin must occur first. Here is where we can take a giant leap forward and miss the context of Paul's writing to the Thessalonians.

Maybe a letter had come or a spirit had prophesied to the contrary that the day of the Lord had arrived. I do think they equated their present persecutions with the tribulation, but the tribulation under the Caesars, especially Nero. Paul says, do not listen to them, even if they say we apostles said it. Jesus mentions in Matthew 24:5, "Many will come in My name saying 'I am Christ' and will deceive many." The great deceiver, the Antichrist, however, had not yet been revealed. With him comes the apostasy as well.

Any message, then, that says the day of the Lord comes before these two events would *not* be from the apostles. They are misleading you. Paul says, "You should not let them deceive you." This is not an imperative command but the aorist subjunctive. The aorist here has the idea of not letting anyone even *begin* to deceive you.

Eve was deceived by the serpent. In 2 Corinthians 11:2 Paul says, "As the serpent deceived Eve ..." and uses the Greek word εξηπατησεν (he deceived). This is the exact word used by Paul in 2 Thessalonians 2:3: μη τις υμας εξαπατηση. Here, the plural *you* is in the emphatic position.

The Greek word in 2 Thessalonians 2:3 and 2 Corinthians 11:2 means "to give a false impression whether by appearance, statement or influence" (Vine 1984, 151). The idea is to deceive thoroughly, completely. This is, unfortunately, what has taken place in the church with regard to Antichrist. Futurism, although partly true, has moved the focus from the Antichrist identified by the Reformers in the 1500s to some future Antichrist who has not yet come. The result is that, like Eve, we are tempted to eat of the forbidden fruit of apostasy and then are carried away into spiritual death. Except for the Holy Spirit in us, this indeed would be the case. We have failed to see, once again, like Eve, our present enemy and the great deceiver. This is the ecumenical movement.

Paul goes on to say that the apostasy and the coming of Antichrist must come prior to the day of the Lord and the rapture. Some try to mix up what Paul means by the day of the Lord. Context tells you what he means. Just because the Thessalonians mixed up the day of the Lord with the tribulation does not mean that Paul did. This is a false assumption by some.

In 2 Thessalonians 2:1, *Paul* calls the day of the Lord, "the coming of our Lord Jesus Christ and our gathering to Him." To attempt to make the day of the Lord identical with the tribulation is the issue that Paul is clearly refuting. "The day of the Lord" mentioned in 2 Thessalonians 2:2 has an article of previous reference and refers back to the event mentioned in 2:1, where the Second Coming and the rapture are coupled together. These two events comprise the day of the Lord. This comes after the tribulation, just as it clearly teaches in Matthew 24:29. Present-day futurists have also followed this error of equating the day of the Lord with the tribulation. Paul did not do that, but he sent this letter to correct the confusion.

The futurist view of Revelation was started by Francisco Ribera in 1591, as part of the counter-Reformation and was taken up by the father of dispensationalism and futurism, John Nelson Darby, who promoted the pretribulation rapture idea. He separated the rapture from the day of the Lord, claiming the latter was the tribulation. So instead of our being raptured from the wrath of God, we were said to be raptured from the tribulation. Zechariah seems to suggest the day of the Lord is a single day.

Zechariah 14:7 says, concerning the day of the Lord, "For it will be a unique day which is known to the Lord, neither day nor night, but it will come about that at evening time there will be light" (NASB). It's a day that Jesus says only the Father knows, a day that is longer than twelve hours, for at evening, there will be light. And on the same day that Lot left Sodom and Gomorrah, it rained fire and brimstone. On the same day that Noah entered the ark, the flood came and took them all away. So shall it be on the day that the Son of Man is revealed. It seems that the day of the Lord must be a literal day, not a seven-year tribulation.

Next, Paul says the man of sin will be revealed. The article is placed before the man of sin so that we might know that Paul is talking about the one-and-only one man of sin. Some think Paul, here, follows what Jesus says in Matthew 24:15: "Therefore when you see the abomination of desolation which was spoken of through Daniel the prophet standing in the holy place (let the reader understand)."

Jesus is talking about the holy place of the temple in Jerusalem, while Paul uses the Greek word ναος for temple as the church, not ιερον, which is the physical temple. Matthew 27:40 says, "You who destroy the temple and rebuild it in three days save Yourself if You are the Son of God, come down from the cross." Here again, ναος is used, by which Jesus always means the temple of His body, the church. He says it in John 2:19: "Destroy this temple and in three days I will raise it up." Then, John explains what Jesus meant by temple in verse 21—εκεινος δε ελεγεν περι του ναου του σωματος αυτου. "And this He said concerning *the temple of His body*" (italics mine).

Paul says in Ephesians 1:22–23, "And He put all things in subjection under His feet, and gave Him as head over all things to *the church which is His body...*" In other words, when Paul uses ναος θεου, he is speaking of the church of God as the temple of God and not the physical Jewish temple in Jerusalem.

Paul, then, is not talking about the abomination of desolation when he describes Antichrist taking his seat in the temple of God in 2

Thessalonians 2:4. *He is talking about the man of sin sitting in the visible church of Christ.* The word for the Jewish temple is ιερov. This word ιερov is used twenty-five times in the book of Acts, and it is always used for this stone temple and never the Greek o ναoς, used for the spiritual temple of the church. This is the huge cover-up that the futurists have aided in keeping.

The futurist interpretation of this passage has never been the interpretation of the Reformers. They held that the book of Revelation must be interpreted historically, and the man of sin was already seated in the temple. According to them, the pope is the man of sin, the son of perdition, who Paul says will take his seat in the temple of God that is the church of Jesus Christ, even as he has done, exalting himself above Christendom. Concerning the papacy, Charles Spurgeon said that no sane man would think anyone but the popes as the man of sin.

In other words, the antichrist is here now, among us, as is the Roman apostasy that denies justification by faith alone and places the so-called vicar of Christ, instead of Christ, as the head of the church. They have believed the lie instead of the truth. This is the apostasy—to turn away from Christ and worship a created being (Satan is an angel), concealed in the Antichrist. This is what Satan tempted Christ to do, trying to get God Himself to worship His own creation—what arrogance. Satan wants us to worship Antichrist and, therefore, the dragon or Satan who dwells in him, as the serpent deceived Eve. Here is the great truth that the Reformers and those before them exposed. Antichrist is now seated in the temple of God, exalting himself above every so-called God or object of worship. Talk about deception.

How do we know this? The first sign Jesus mentions in Matthew 24:5 is, "Many will come in My name saying I am Christ."

First John 2:18 also follows Matthew's account:

> Children it is the last hour; and just as you heard that
> antichrist is coming, even now many antichrists have
> arisen; from this we know that it is the last hour.

Jesus's own words tell us what John means by Antichrist; namely, someone saying, "I am Christ." Both passages mention "many antichrists," and the last hour is the last hour before the night begins. In John 9:4, Jesus says (in the Greek), ερχεται νυξ—"night is coming." The same is said in 1 John 2:18 (in Greek), αντιχριστος ερχεται—"antichrist is coming." This is the final Antichrist, when he comes riding on a white horse, according to Revelation 6:2.

Antichrist coming is like the arrival of the white horse and the first sign of Jesus. But has not Paul claimed that Antichrist now sits in the temple of God? Indeed, but the final Antichrist is the one who comes like the rider on the white horse. He comes as a peacemaker, having a bow and wearing a white robe. He wears a victor's crown of some recent victory. But he comes to Israel with a covenant of peace. Without the state of Israel, like the futurists say, no covenant. But all the popes are Antichrist—many will come in My name, many Antichrists, and the last one will come and make a covenant with the nation of Israel and set up a peace deal for the building of the temple. The present pope Francis could be the last one. Next year could be when it takes place.

John says that the fact there are many Antichrists is the indication that it is "the last hour" before the night comes, before Antichrist comes riding on a white horse—the first horseman and the first sign Jesus mentions. In other words, we need to be looking for Antichrist as someone who says, "I am Christ." Muslims or Buddhists don't claim to be Christ. This is a Christian apostasy because Antichrist says, "I am Christ." Only the papacy has been calling itself the vicar of Christ, ever since AD 493, when Pope Gelasius I began the precedent (Wikipedia, "Gelasius I").

You cannot be called an apostate by being a Buddhist or Muslim or an adherent to Judaism because they never were Christians from the beginning (Lenski 1946, 407).

R. C. H. Lenski (1946), in his commentary on 2 Thessalonians 2:3, says,

> The fact that this apostasy will occur in the Christian church is beyond question; it would otherwise not be an "apostasy." The man of the lawlessness will be its head. Yet some have thought of a Jewish apostasy, the Jewish national rejection of Christ, and also of the Jewish

> political apostasy from Rome. Others think of a general
> moral falling away from such standards of morality as
> existed in the pagan world. (407)

Clearly, we are talking about a visible apostasy and man of sin, which would happen in the church and is now history. No wonder the four creatures say, "Come and see." History is proof that the pope is Antichrist because history reveals the prophecy of Paul in 2 Thessalonians 2:3–4. They don't say "Come and listen, but come and see what is already history. This is only revealed at the end.

Martin Luther, like many of the Reformers, took on the historicist view of Revelation and especially about what Paul says in 2 Thessalonians 2. Luther believed that Antichrist had already taken his seat in the temple of God, meaning the church.

Jesus says, "For many will come in My name saying I am Christ and shall deceive many" (Matthew 24:5 KJV). According to Wycliffe, the "many" refers to the many popes who have claimed to be the vicar of Christ. Only the papacy has made the claim to be God or Jesus Christ on the earth, the vicar of Christ, the Holy Father. *Many popes have said, "I am the vicar of Christ."* The first sign mentioned by Jesus is the same white horse in Revelation 6:2.

Pope Francis has been one of the most productive popes in the ecumenical movement. He has travelled all over the world even to Japan in 2019. This is the rider on the white horse, wearing a white garment and carrying his message of peace—the bow without an arrow. Next stop, Israel?

What is his goal? To rally the whole world and apostate Christianity against the saints and to make war with the Lamb and His army (Revelation 19:19). God had a response to the work of the man of sin. What follows the white horse is the red horse of war and the black horse of famine; then, the pale horse of pestilence. The COVID-19 pandemic is not a coincidence.

The pope visited the far east in early 2019 and negotiated with China, reaching out to them. But the pandemic began in China and was most severe in Italy and Spain, two papal vassals. Those who participate in the sins of Babylon will also receive of her plagues (Revelation 18:4). Is this a warning, especially to Israel, who, since 2014, has begun to negotiate for peace in Jerusalem through the Vatican? This all fits in with the new ecumenism promoted by Francis and all faiths in Jerusalem in unity.

For this reason I think the pope's next stop is Israel. This would begin the final week and the building of the temple. The plagues of war, famine, and pestilence would then come upon Israel after she is duped into making some kind of covenant with Rome. Jesus said to the Jews, "I have come in My Father's name and you do not receive Me; if another will come in his own name, you will receive him" (John 5:43). The popes have claimed to be the Holy Father. Antichrist denies the Father and the Son by claiming to be both. He comes in his own name. In 2014, Pope Francis was seen "standing" at the holy place, the western wall of the Jewish temple. The Jews also showed him a projected copy of a temple they would like to build. Peace and safety! A sign of things to come, indeed. Once you know who Antichrist is, the rest is rather clear.

Another point is that the word *anti*, in Greek, is also translated as *vicarious* in Latin. The root form of this word is *vicar*, as in vicar of Christ or antichrist. *Vicarious* means substitution, just as *anti* has the idea of substitution, meaning "in place of," rather than "against," as we translate it today (Hunt, 1994, 45).

Not even Hitler, or Napoleon, or Stalin, or the Caesars said, "I am Christ," but the popes have made this declaration of vicar of Christ from as early as Pope Gelasius I (492–496). Jesus says many will come, saying, "I am Christ," but really, only the papacy makes this blasphemy.

Some say, "Well, this is only one man, but there were many different popes." Yes, but they all have said, "I am Christ." Even though they are different people, they all are included in one dynasty, and they all sit in the same seat. This seat, which Paul mentions with the Greek verb, καθιξω—"I sit"—is the aorist infinitive καθισαι—"to sit"—and is the word for *cathedral*. Infinitives often complete important ideas in Greek (Mounce, 2009, 298).

Paul is making an important point about this seat, which has the idea of permanency because of the aorist tense (Lenski 1946, 410). The important idea Paul is making by using the infinitive is the permanency of this seat, denoted by the aorist. Also, this seat has been and still is in Rome, the seat which the dragon gives to the beast from the sea. It has been there for more than fourteen hundred years and not at some future time during the tribulation. Papal worship is just pagan worship. What we have is the apostasy and the man of sin. Matthew 24:15 has him standing, not sitting. Paul has Antichrist sitting in the church well before the day of the Lord. This is the woman who puts leaven in the meal until it becomes totally leavened. Jesus says this is what the kingdom of God is like—apostate Christianity headed up in the pope.

While it is tempting here to make the woman in Revelation 17 the Roman Catholic Church and exclude America, we need to really understand Revelation. The image of Daniel and the chronology of the beasts in Revelation 12,13 and 17 make Babylon more than just a church. Chapter 18 calls this city an economic giant. Hardly descriptive of the Roman Catholic Church. We need to read Jeremiah 50,51 to see what John is describing in Revelation 18. The key to the woman in Revelation 17 is that she is identical to the Babylon of Revelation 18 being clothed in purple, and scarlet, and adorned with gold. The Roman Catholic Church is not an economic power. If she fell none of the merchants of the earth would weep. Another key point of the woman in Revelation 17 is that John is shown this woman just before her judgment. That judgment is described in Revelation 18:10 "for in one hour your judgment has come." Therefore, the woman of 17:3 riding the beast is the commercial Babylon destroyed by fire in chapter 18. Psalm 137:8 says, "O daughter of Babylon who art to be destroyed." (KJV) This is America not the Roman Catholic Church.

As I have said the two legs of iron are portrayed in the book of Revelation in the dragon and the beast from the sea. These legs are identical because they are both Rome, imperial and Papal. Now Papal Rome as the beast from the sea is all iron. Throughout the middle ages it was iron. But just before her judgment the woman appears riding this same sea beast, now a scarlet beast. This is the iron and the clay in the feet of Daniel's image. But the clay corresponds in Revelation with the beast from the earth. We have shown that the beast from the earth arises after the beast from the sea, the second leg terminates in the dissolution of the Holy Roman Empire, in 1805. Then does the beast receive a deadly wound when the pope is removed from Rome and devested of his temporal power. This is the deadly wound.

Just when the pope loses his temporal power in 1798, America arises as the beast from the earth. The two beasts will then merge in chapter 17 of Revelation as the woman riding the scarlet beast. This is the iron and the clay in Daniel's image. The feet are the end of days merger of the woman riding the scarlet beast. The scarlet beast is the eighth the head healed. America is the woman, Babylon. Even today we see this merger taking place. Together they will attack Israel and over come them.

The Reformers believed this woman to be the Roman Catholic Church because the beast from the earth had not yet appeared.

Now if we look briefly at Psalm 137:7,8 we have a text which may shed some light on our dilemma of who is Babylon. The Psalm begins with "By the rivers of Babylon, there we sat down and wept, when we remembered Zion. Upon the willows in the midst of it we hung our harps. For there our captors demanded of us songs, and our tormentors mirth saying, "Sing us one of the songs of Zion.""

This is the Babylonian captivity of 586 BC when Judah was taken into captivity to Babylon. Now this psalms also states *the coming judgment of Babylon* even as Revelation 17 describes in a vision the judgment of the woman riding the scarlet beast.

Here is what it says. "Remember O Lord, the children of Edom in the day of Jerusalem; who said, Rase *it*, rase *it*, *even* to the foundation thereof. O daughter of Babylon, who art to be destroyed; happy *shall he be*, that rewardeth thee as thou hast served us." (Psalm 137:7,8 KJV).

Now Edom means red and refers to Rome, here Rome is the scarlet beast even as the red dragon. But the woman is called the daughter of Babylon. The daughter of Babylon is to be destroyed even as Revelation 18 describes her destruction. The Babylon of Revelation 18 is commercial Babylon and seems to fit with the daughter of Babylon since she is destroyed in one day by fire according to Revelation 18:8. This is not the Roman Catholic Church.

Our dilemma then of who is Babylon seems to suggest we have Rome as the mother and America as the daughter of Babylon. This latter Babylon whose judgment we see in Revelation 18 must certainly be the woman who rides the beast, the daughter of Babylon. Edom is the scarlet beast. Here we have the two beasts joined together in the destruction of Jerusalem.

For this reason, John says in Revelation 18:2 "Fallen, fallen is Babylon the Great," because both these beasts are Babylon. Each will be judged. Rome as the mother, the iron (scarlet beast) and America as the daughter, in the clay or the beast from the earth. This is the daughter of Babylon riding the scarlet beast. The children of Edom may be the Roman Catholic Church. Those who worship the beast and his image. This is the apostate church and it is Rome who introduces *the leaven* into the kingdom of God. In the next chapter we will get a better picture of this apostasy.

7

The Little Horn and His Boasts

In the late Middle Ages and in the wake of the Protestant Reformation, accusations of being the Antichrist were levied against the Pope. Amidst the controversy, Francisco Ribera in 1585 began writing a lengthy (500 page) commentary on the Book of Revelation, titled In Sacrum Beati Ioannis Apostoli, & Evangelistiae Apocalypsin Commentarii, proposing that the first chapters of the Apocalypse applied to ancient pagan Rome, and the rest referred to a yet future period of 3½ literal years, immediately prior to the second coming. (Wikipedia, "Francisco Ribera")

By placing the Antichrist of Revelation into the final three and a half years, the Jesuits were able to counter the Reformation claim that the pope was the historical Antichrist of Revelation 13. Unfortunately, this futurist view has been received by many today, including me—for a time. Futurism is correct in that there is a future final week. It is just what they have missed in the book of Revelation in shoving all things to the end. Here are some quotes from various sources on their blasphemous statements:

Cardinal Sarto, who became Pope Pius X, said, "The Pope represents Jesus Christ Himself" (Cardinal Sarto 1896, 11).

If this is not what they think, then why not write a statement denying this claim? Because when the popes say something, they are infallible, so it cannot be changed.

Pope Leo XIII said the following about the role of the papacy and the Roman Church:

> Our thoughts went out towards the immense multitude of those who are strangers to the gladness that filled all Catholic hearts: some because they lie in absolute ignorance of the Gospel; others because they dissent from the Catholic belief, though they bear the name of Christians.
>
> This thought has been, and is, a source of deep concern to Us; for it is impossible to think of such a large portion of mankind deviating, as it were, from the right path, as they move away from Us, and not experience a sentiment of innermost grief. But since We hold upon this earth the place of God Almighty … (*Praeclara Gratulationis Publicae*, or *The Reunion of Christendom* 1894, para 5)

Unfortunately, none of the popes deny these blasphemies; in fact, at times they say them themselves.

> The Pope and God are the same, so he has all power in Heaven and earth. (Pope Pius V, quoted in Barclay, "Cities Petrus Bertanous," 218)
>
> All names which in the Scriptures are applied to Christ, by virtue of which it is established that He is over the church, all the same names are applied to the Pope. (*On the Authority of the Councils*, book 2, chapter 17)

Now concerning this changing of laws the popes have changed the atonement and redemptive work of Christ into a dual affair with Mary as together with Christ redeeming the human race.

Benedict XV, Litterae Apostolicae, *Inter Sodalicia*, March 22, 1918, AAS 10, 1918, 182: "... the fact that she was with Him crucified and dying, was in accord with the divine plan. For with her suffering and dying Son, Mary endured suffering and almost death. She gave up her Mother's rights over her Son to procure the salvation of mankind, and to appease the divine justice, she, as much as she could, immolated her Son, so that one can truly affirm that together with Christ she has redeemed the human race. (Benedict XV, Inter Sodalicia, 1918)

Part of their apostasy is to make Mary a co-redeemer with Christ. Mary represents the image of the beast, which many will worship. But the same fate will come to them all. (Revelation 14:9–10)

Papal infallibility is another one of their blasphemies. The Bible declares that "all have sinned and come short of the glory of God" (Roman 3:23). This includes the pope and Mary. These boasts of the papacy fulfill the Bible's prediction of what the little horn's power would do:

And he shall speak great words against the Most High, and shall wear out the saints of the Most High, and think to change times and laws ... (Daniel 7:25)

And there was given unto him a mouth speaking great things and blasphemies; and power was given unto him to continue forty and two months. And he opened his mouth in blasphemy against God, to blaspheme his name, and his tabernacle, and them that dwell in heaven (Revelation 13:5–6)

In Daniel 7:8, we read about the little horn, and, like the beast of Revelation 13:5, this little horn will speak boastful words, and he will have eyes like the eyes of a man. This may be a reference to what is called a bishop, which in the Greek is an overseer. The papacy is also called the

Holy See. A *see* is a bishopric. An overseer is a bishop, like the bishop of Rome.

But this little horn with eyes has elevated himself to be an apostle; then Peter, the chief apostle; and finally, the vicar of Christ Himself, and now God. These are the blasphemes against God that come from their own mouths. By unashamedly taking this seat, he shows himself to be God and accepts the worship of his followers. For a man to accept worship as God is blaspheme. To claim to forgive sins, which only God can do, is also blasphemy. Jesus did because He is God.

This little horn comes out of the fourth beast, and that fourth beast, we know, is Rome. The papacy is in Rome and, therefore, comes out of Rome. The little horn comes up after the ten horns, which also come up out of the fourth beast. Yet the little horn shall be different from the ten (Daniel 7:24). While a king, like the other horns, this little horn is also the bishop of Rome and ultimately claims both ecclesiastical and political authority.

At this point, I would like to look at the man on the white horse in Revelation 6:2, as it relates to the little horn. The text says, "And I looked and behold a white horse and he who sat on it had a bow and a crown was given to him and he went out conquering and to conquer." Christ, as the Lamb, is the only one worthy to open the seals of the book. Jesus alone can then explain the white horse.

> The disciples came to Him privately, saying "Tell us what will be the sign of Your coming and of the end of the age?" And Jesus answered and said to them, "See to it that *no man deceives you*. For many will come in My name saying "I am Christ" and shall deceive many." (Matthew 24:3–5 KJV)

This is precisely what Paul says in 2 Thessalonians 2:3:

> *Let no man deceive you* by any means: for that day shall not come, except there come a falling away first, and that man of sin be revealed, the son of perdition. (KJV)

This is the succession of the popes, and it pictures a dynasty or a throne, just as Daniel 7 clearly depicts the little horn as a continuation of the fourth beast. Rome fell in AD 476, but out of that kingdom, the papacy grew, and today, it is still the fourth king. These are the two legs of iron. This little horn is the same fourth king of Daniel 11:36—"Then the king will do as he pleases and *he will exalt and magnify himself above every god.*" This is exactly what Paul says of Antichrist in 2 Thessalonians 2:4: "*Who opposes and exalts himself above every so-called god* or object of worship so that he takes his seat in the temple of God displaying himself as being God."

According to Daniel 7:8, this little horn would arise after the fourth beast, which fell in AD 476 and the ten horns arose. The pope took his seat in Rome and by the 8th century had temporal power. He began to extend this authority to the horns by crowning the emperors of the Holy Roman Empire, beginning with Charlemagne in AD 800. What restrained him from taking his seat was imperial Rome itself. Until Constantine moved from Rome to Constantinople the beast was restrained.

He was not restrained by the Holy Spirit but the Roman Empire itself and the Caesars seated. Paul talks of the restrainer as first a thing and then a person. The thing holding him back was the Roman Empire. Acts 17:7 says that while at Thessalonica, Paul and Silas were accused of acting contrary to the decrees of Caesar. Paul had to write covertly to the Thessalonians, in light of the sensitive situation at Thessalonica. The little horn comes up after the ten horns, which, in turn, came out of the fourth beast, Imperial Rome. This seat was in Rome, but this could not take place until the Caesars who sat on that throne in Rome were taken away. Emperor Constantine moved his seat from Rome to Byzantium in AD 330.

Here is why Paul shifts from the gender neutral to the masculine with regard to the restrainer. The Roman Empire, with the Caesars *seated in Rome*, was the *thing* holding this rise of the little horn, and Constantine was the man who moved his seat from Rome to Constantinople.

The rise of Papal Rome then is the second leg of iron in the image of Daniel chapter two. The restrainer, both as a power and then as a man, had to exit that seat in Rome. Many see the deadly wound of one of the heads of the beast as the fall of Rome in 476. But this cannot be because this wound belongs to the dragons head, but the one in 1798 is to the head of the beast from the sea, the second leg. The wound refers to the fall of the Holy Roman Empire in 1805 and the removal of temporal power in 1798. The wound is on the beast from the sea, Papal Rome. The wound heals because the iron reappears in the feet of the image as an eighth.

This little horn, then, is a continuation of the fourth kingdom, and he will reign until Christ returns to destroy him. The little horn is the Antichrist but is a dynasty of many Antichrists, just as each pope takes the same single seat. Each successive pope represents the fourth king, the beast of Rome.

How does this reign take place? Each pope reigns in the political seat of Rome and in the seat mentioned by Paul, in the temple of God, as the successor of Peter. The political power of the little horn is exercised through its vassals, the kings of the earth, who submit to Roman Catholicism and the headship of the pope. The ten horns are a part of this, no doubt. Those kings, or countries, who will submit to Rome by concordats or ambassadors of the Vatican are supported through elections and political alliances. These were the crowned kings of the Holy Roman Empire.

Those Protestant nations that did not submit to the headship of the Roman pontiff were either excommunicated, or overthrown from within, or, if necessary, deposed by war. In the 1500s, England, under Queen Elizabeth I, took a Protestant stand. She rejected the pope as head of the church and king of kings and was repeatedly threatened with assassination (Grattan, 1887, 59). This was the Old World order, before the time when Napoleon finally inflicted the deadly wound on the beast's head and defeated the last king of the Holy Roman Empire in 1805.

Napoleon had the pope removed from Rome for a short time in 1798, and France removed all temporal power from the pope. This is the deadly wound when Pope Pius VI died in 1799 but this would be healed when Pope Pius VII returned to Rome in 1814. Power was returned to the popes through the Lateran Treaty when Mussolini gave Vatican City to the pope. Both these are the rise of the eighth head, and is the scarlet beast of Revelation 17. The European Union are the soon to be crowned horns, are the ten kings who will receive power one hour with the beast.

What happened immediately after the concordat with Italy and dominion was restored to the little horn? He made a concordat with Nazi Germany and fascist Spain, which plunged the world into World War II. After the white horse comes the red. When it looked like Russia and Communism was going to take over Europe, after Germany stumbled at Stalingrad, Rome made a change of alliances, and turned to America her daughter. Suddenly, Italy was invaded, and a new alliance was in the making.

The popes call themselves King of kings, and try to carry out this rule, even as the fourth kingdom continues today to have dominion over the whole earth, as it says in Daniel 7:23.

The new world order today is just the old world order, revived in the scarlet beast and now with America riding the beast. As the beast from the sea, the popes persecuted monarchs such as Queen Elizabeth I and other Protestant kings and queens who would not bow to Rome (Grattan, 1887, 59). The Anglo-Spanish war of 1585–1604 was Rome's attempt to bring down Protestant England through Spain, an obedient vassal to the papacy.

Many of the wars of Europe were the attempts by this power to exert its dominion in certain unwilling countries. It can start civil wars, sedition, and division in order to force these nations to bow to her rule, especially when it comes to snuffing out heretics. The new world order which is just emerging with the feet of iron and clay will be no different from the old, except that she uses different nations today. If our analysis is correct then America may be one of those nations. This new world order I believe is pictured in the woman riding the beast.

The European Union we believe are the ten horns of the beast and part of the feet in Daniel's image. The iron and the clay, I believe, are the two beasts in Revelation 13. They are represented in the scarlet beast riding the woman. These are the sons of Edom and the daughter of Babylon. We are not excluding world religion in this scene since the apostasy is linked to the man of sin. The pope is still the man of sin and his religion the apostasy.

The preamble of the writers of the King James Version of the Bible notes that "by writing in defense of the truth, (which hath given such a blow unto that Man of Sin as will not be healed)." But he is still seated in the temple of God and will do so until Christ returns to slay the beast.

The Westminster Confession of Faith (1646) states,

> There is no other head of the church but the Lord Jesus Christ, nor can the Pope of Rome in any sense be head thereof, but is that antichrist, that *man of sin*, and *son of perdition*, that *exalts himself* in *the church* against Christ and all that is called God. (chapter 25, point 6)

This confession is taken right out of 2 Thessalonians 2:3–4, as you can clearly see by the words I have put in italics. They believed the temple of God—ο ναος του θεου—was really the church of God, not the Jewish temple, which is the word το ιερον.

John Wesley, the founder of the Methodist Church, stated, "The Pope is the son of perdition, as he has caused the death of numberless multitudes, both of his opposers and followers, destroyed innumerable souls, and will himself perish everlastingly" (*Explanatory Notes upon the New Testament*, 2 Thessalonians 2:3). Here are some famous quotes that support the apostles. Paul's prophecy is 2 Thessalonians 2:3–4 of the Antichrist.

Tertullian

> He who now hinders must hinder until he be taken out of the way. What obstacle is there but the Roman State; the falling away of which, by being scattered into ten kingdoms, shall introduce antichrist. (Tertullian, "On the Resurrection," chapters 24–25. Christian apologist in North Africa, AD 200)

Here are the early church fathers, declaring what the restrainer represents and how the little horn would emerge out of the Roman state, after being scattered into ten kingdoms.

John Chrysostom

> Only there is one that restrains now, until he be taken
> out of the way, that is when the Roman Empire is taken
> out of the way, then he [Antichrist] shall come. (John
> Chrysostom Homily on 2 Thessalonians 2, Number 4.
> Bishop of Constantinople, AD 390)

Now concerning the restrainer who is taken out of the way, we have
the following quote from Edward B. Elliot:

> We have the consenting testimony of the early
> fathers, from Irenaeus, the disciple of St. John, down
> to Chrysostom and Jerome, to the effect that it was
> understood to be imperial power ruling and residing at
> Rome. (Elliot, 1862, 92)

Reformer Martin Luther

> I know that the pope is Antichrist, and that his seat is
> that of Satan himself.

> The papacy is a general chase, by command of the
> Roman Pontiff, for the purpose of running. (Bainton
> 1950, pp. 153-155)

The little horn, then, who arises after the ten horns is clearly the
man of sin, who sits in the temple of God and exalts himself as God.
They are one and the same, both political and apostate, as Revelation 17
combines the two with the woman riding the beast. This is so because
the woman is also Rome, the mother of harlots. She is drunk with the
blood of the saints.

According to *Foxe's Book of Martyrs*, from 1200 to 1800, many
Christians died for their faith. What persecuting power was responsible
for this holocaust? History does not lie, and this power is not a future
power but a very present one. Neither is it a past one only, such as the

Caesars of Rome, because Rome fell in 476, and these persecutions did not cease with imperial Rome. Rome is the woman as well.

Here are some of the places where figures about religious persecutions are given. Dowling, in his *History of Romanism*, says:

> From the birth of Popery in 607 to the present time, it is estimated by careful and credible historians, that more than fifty million of the human family, have been slaughtered for the crime of heresy by popish persecutors, an average of more than forty thousand religious murders for every year of the existence of popery. (Dowling, 1871, 541–42)

This is a conservative estimate, as one can find more quotes where the numbers are greater.

Where do the futurists get the idea that this little horn will only make war with the saints at the end of the age? Daniel 7:21–22 says,

> I kept looking and that horn was waging war with *the saints* and overpowering them UNTIL the Ancient of Days came and judgment was passed in favor of *the saints* of the Highest One and the time arrived when the saints took possession of the kingdom.

Church history gives us the true picture. Rome is drunk with the blood of *the saints* and of the blood of the witnesses of Jesus (Revelation 17:6). This is something that we can see now in history, not in some distant future. Futurist interpretation of Revelation, as noted earlier, was part of the Roman Catholic counter-Reformation to cover up the deeds of the papacy and to prevent Christians from identifying the real Antichrist.

In conclusion, there is really only one point we need to realize in this entire discussion. According to the apostle Paul, in 2 Thessalonians 2:4, Antichrist is sitting in the church now.

Paul would not make that kind of a mistake in the Greek if he meant the Jewish temple. Paul is saying that before the Second Coming of Christ, there will arise Antichrist in the church of God, who will exalt himself above all and take his seat permanently in this church, showing himself to be Christ's equal. This can only be the papacy. He is the Antichrist, not a future political leader, as we are being taught today. The beast from the sea is both a kingdom and an individual. From the 8th century the popes in succession have each one occupied the seat of antichrist and remained there until the deadly wound in 1798. This is the little horn, having temporal power, for a millennia and then regaining it again as an eighth head. First as an individual in 1814 and then as the scarlet beast in 1929. Antichrist is a dynasty.

This is what Luther, John Knox, Thomas Cranmer, John Calvin, John Huss, Tyndale, Charles Spurgeon, Sir Isaac Newton, the Westminster Confession, the Baptist Confession of 1689, and many others came to realize from the apostles' account in 2 Thessalonians 2:4. They all, with one voice, say that the pope is the man of sin, the son of perdition, which the apostle Paul describes in 2 Thessalonians 2:4.

Far be it from us, then, to say anything different, especially in light of the souls of those who were slain because of the word of their testimony, which they had maintained, and who still cry out with a loud voice, saying, "How long O Lord holy and true wilt Thou refrain from judging and avenging our blood on those who dwell on the earth? (Revelation 6:9–10). History records their voices, which cannot be denied. The pope is the only possible man of sin of 2 Thessalonians 2:3, which, indeed, no sane man can deny. (Spurgeon).

To sum up this section, the beast from the sea is both a kingdom and a king. This is Papal Rome the second leg of iron in Daniel's image. The dragon is the first leg of iron and represents imperial Rome. These two legs each last for at least a thousand years. Imperial Rome began to emerge by 264 BC with the Punic Wars against Carthage and continued even until the popes secured temporal power in the 8th century. Then the Holy Roman Empire emerged as the second leg of iron and lasted from AD 800 with Charlemagne until 1805 when Napoleon defeated Francis II the last emperor of Papal Rome. At this same time the popes lost their temporal power and were cast out of Rome. However, like the unclean spirit they returned to the house and although the idol had fallen it was set up again only to be broken at the end.

The feet of Daniel's image then is the merger of the beast from the sea which recovers and the beast from the land, America. She is the beast from the earth because she began at the same time the beast of the sea was ending. This is John's chronology with the dragon, the beast from the sea, the beast from the earth and finally the scarlet beast, with the woman riding on its back. This final part is a union between the sea beast and the land beast. This is the feet of iron and clay in Daniel's image.

We do not however exclude Rome as Babylon since both these beasts must represent Babylon, Rome as the mother and America as the daughter of Babylon. Religious Babylon should be connected to the mother, Rome, and must include her children. These are the children of Edom, who worship the beast and his image and gladly take his mark.

To say we understand this would be far from the truth. However, the picture is still summed up in the woman riding the beast in Revelation 17. Here is the final world order at the return of Christ. This is America as the daughter of Babylon heading up the G7 joined with antichrist the scarlet beast (Edom) heading up the European Union. These two beasts will make war with Israel and overcome them. Russia and China are not part of the feet revealed in Daniel's image. The scarlet beast and the ten kings will turn on the harlot and with the aid of Russia and China destroy the daughter of Babylon. Therefore, the warning in Revelation 18:4 is to come out of Babylon, near the end of the tribulation.

8

Does the Rapture Appear in Matthew 24?

Moving along to the Second Coming and our rapture, some are teaching today that there is no rapture. These adherents go to the passage in Matthew 24:37–39 where Jesus says,

> For the coming of the Son of Man will be just like the days of Noah. For as in those days which were before the flood they were eating and drinking they were marrying and giving in marriage until the day that Noah entered the ark, and did not understand until the flood came and took them all away, so shall the coming of the Son of Man be.

Then they say, well, this is talking about the Parousia of Christ for judgment, but this passage is not the rapture. They are right that this is not a rapture passage. As in the days of Noah, everyone who was taken away by the flood was lost. Only those left behind were saved, like Noah, his family, and the animals. Jesus says, in Matthew 24:40, "Then there shall be two men in the field; one will be taken and one will be left, two women will be grinding at the mill, one will be taken and one will be left." This is not the rapture. These are taken away in judgment just as those in Noah's day were taken away by the flood. But the rapture is before the judgment so we should look at verses before Matthew 24:40.

But why not read Matthew 24:31? "And He will send forth His angels with a great trumpet and they will gather together His elect from the four winds from one end of the sky to the other." Is this not the rapture of the church just before the judgment? Paul describes this in 1 Thessalonians 4:17 and 2 Thessalonians 2:1.

In fact, the Greek word for *gather together* in 2 Thessalonians 2:1 is the same word used in Matthew 24:31—"and they will gather together."

What, then, is Jesus talking about when He says, "then there shall be two men in the field one will be taken and one will be left" (Matthew 24:40). To be left is to be left alive and not swept away with the judgment. But few men will be left out of the huge population of the earth who are not a part of the raptured church. Just as in the days of Noah, when there were more animals in the ark than people, so in the day the Son of Man is revealed, there will be more animals left alive than people.

This is just like it says in Isaiah 24:4–6:

> The earth mourns and withers the world fades and withers the exalted of the people of the earth fade away. The earth is also polluted by its inhabitants, for they transgressed laws, violated statutes, broke the everlasting covenant. Therefore, a curse devours the earth and those who live in it are held guilty. *Therefore, the inhabitants of the earth are burned and few men are left.* (italics mine)

This is what Jesus is talking about, when, at His coming like in the days of Lot, they were eating and drinking and did not understand until Lot left Sodom and Gomorrah, and fire came down from heaven and burned them up. The few left in Lot's day were Lot and his two daughters; the rest were destroyed. The few left in Noah's day were Noah and seven others of his family. This will be the same when the Son of Man comes back. Only a few, compared to the vast population of this world, will be left. The judgment will be universal—men, women, creditors, debtors, farmers, newlyweds; all who are still in the flesh will be judged by fire. But just before this, the church, who are not in the flesh, will be raptured away by the angels, as Lot was taken away from Sodom by the two angels while the Lord Himself waited with Abraham.

Likewise, Christ will descend from heaven and send forth His angels, and we will be caught up by those angels to meet Him in the air.

The same is true of Noah and his family. On the very day Noah entered the ark, the flood came and took the rest away. The entering into the ark is compared to the five wise virgins, entering the wedding feast. This too is the rapture. When our new bodies are given, we will be one flesh with Christ and married to Him forever. For the two shall become one flesh. This is at the rapture.

Those who say there is no rapture and that Jesus does not talk about the rapture in Matthew 24 either cannot read or have selective vision, for the rapture of the church is clearly portrayed in Matthew 24:31 and, as the context makes it clear, before 24:40, where two men will be in the field, one taken and one left. Those who are left have no change of body but go into the millennium in the flesh. These are the ones who will repopulate the world during the millennium, just as Noah and his family did after the flood. Those who are worthy of attaining that age and the resurrection from the dead neither marry nor are given in marriage. So the church is not involved in procreation anymore.

We shall reign with Christ for a thousand years over what is left of humanity, those who didn't take the mark and were spared from the wrath of God, which was poured out on all who would take the mark of the beast or worship the beast or his image. For this reason, we also need to tell humanity the gospel, for them to be saved, but we also need to warn them as to who the Antichrist is and not to worship him or take his mark. The Reformers preached justification by faith, but they also exposed antichrist, who they believed, to be the Roman pontiff who sits in the temple of God. There is a dire judgment for worshipping the beast and taking the mark. Warnings are necessary as well.

Back to the rapture in Matthew 24. We should not be surprised then that this teaching of no rapture in Matthew 24:40 has begun to emerge. In order to defend the pretribulation rapture theory, their adherents have divorced the rapture from Matthew 24 altogether, saying Matthew was written only to the Jews, not the church. By taking such a stand, they are now unable to defend against a no-rapture argument. Without a text there is no argument.

How can they defend against a no-rapture theory in Matthew

24:38–41, when dispensationalists claim there is no rapture in Matthew's Olivet discourse? To say this was only written for the Jews and not the church, is completely ludicrous. The Olivet discourse is in Luke and Mark as well.

Nevertheless, the Lord is true, and He has not left us without the rapture. Matthew 24:29 says,

> But immediately *after the tribulation* of those days the sun will be darkened and the moon will not give its light and the stars will fall from the sky and the powers of the heavens will be shaken and then the sign of the Son of Man will appear in the sky and then all the tribes of the earth will mourn, and they will see the Son of Man coming on the clouds of the sky with power and great glory, *and he will send forth his angels with a great trumpet and they will gather together his elect from the four winds from one end of the sky to the other.* (italics mine)

If this is not the rapture, then we might as well toss out the whole Bible. The rapture is not before but plainly after the tribulation, just as Jesus says. To deny this is to deny the plain, historical, grammatical interpretation of scripture. This rapture is what delivers us from the wrath to come (1 Thessalonians 1:10).

This wrath is spoken about in Isaiah 34:1–5:

> Draw near O nations to hear; and listen O peoples! For the Lord's indignation is against all the nations, And His wrath against all their armies; He has utterly destroyed them, He has given them over to slaughter. So, their slain will be thrown out, and their corpses will give off their stench. And the mountains will be drenched with their blood. And all the *host of heaven will wear away*, and the *sky will be rolled up like a scroll*; All their hosts will also wither away as a leaf withers from the vine, or as one withers from the fig tree. For My sword is satiated

in heaven, behold it shall descend for judgment upon Edom. And upon the people whom I have devoted to destruction.

This is certainly speaking about Revelation 19, where Christ slays the beast and the kings of the earth. *Edom* means red. This is the scarlet beast with seven heads and ten horns. Remember the woman Babylon is destroyed by fire, not from the Lord but by the beast and the ten kings.

Look too at some comparisons to Matthew 24:29, where the stars will fall from the sky, and 24:30, where the sign of the Son of Man appears. This sign of the Son of Man, according to early church fathers, is the "rolling back of the heavens like a scroll." Clearly, we are looking at the outpouring of God's wrath at the Second Coming of Christ. This is after the tribulation of those days, and the wrath is distinct from the tribulation. In the Didache IV, The Lord Is Coming, it reads:

In the last days, false prophets and corrupters will multiply, and the sheep will turn into wolves, and love will be turned into hate. As lawlessness increases, men will hate and persecute and betray one another.

And then the *Deceiver of the world* will appear as a son of God, and *will do signs and wonders,* and the earth will be delivered into his hands. He will commit abominations which have never been seen since the world began. Then all mankind will come to the fire of testing, and many will fail and perish. But those who endure in their faith will be saved by him who was accursed. And then shall the signs of the truth appear: *first a sign of a rift in the heavens,* then a sign of a *voice of a trumpet,* and *thirdly* the resurrection of the dead. Yet not of all, but as it was said:

The Lord shall come and all his saints with him. Then shall the world see the Lord coming upon the clouds of heaven with power and dominion to repay each man

according to his works, with justice, before all men and
the angels. Amen. (Ante-Nicene Fathers 1995, p.382)

The voice of the trumpet mentioned here in the Didache is certainly
taken from Matthew 24:31—"And He will send forth His angels with a
great trumpet." Also, Paul's account in 1 Thessalonians 4:16: "For the
Lord Himself will descend from heaven with a shout with the voice of
the archangel; and with *the trumpet of God*; and *the dead in Christ shall
rise first.*" (italics mine).

The resurrection follows the trumpet, just as it does in the Didache.
Compare the order in the Didache with Matthew 24. First, the rift of
the heavens: sign of the Son of Man; second, the trumpet: angels with
trumpets; third, the resurrection of the dead, with the gathering of
the elect from the four winds. This is the same order as Paul has in 1
Thessalonians 4:16—first, the descent of the Lord from heaven; second,
the trumpet; and third, the dead in Christ rising first. These three each
line up perfectly. Therefore, as it says in Matthew 24:29, these signs
follow the tribulation.

Now as we see Edom destroyed according to Isaiah 34, Babylon must
fall before this but at the end of the tribulation. In Isaiah 13:9 it says,
"Behold, the day of the Lord is coming, cruel, with fury and burning
anger, to make the land a desolation; and He will exterminate its sinners
from it. For the stars of heaven and their constellations will not flash
forth their light; *the sun will be dark when it rises, and the moon will not
shed its light.*" (italics mine).

This prophecy is concerning the daughter of Babylon. Now the
reason the sun will be dark when it rises and the moon not shed its
light, is because of the smoke from the burning of Babylon. Smoke can
darken the sun and the moon and the stars. "The merchants of these
things who became rich from her, will stand at a distance because of
the fear of her torment, weeping and mourning....v.18 and were crying
out as they saw the smoke of her burning, saying, What city is like the
great city?" (Revelation 18:15,18). America is the daughter of Babylon
who art to be destroyed.

9

Revelation 13 and America's Role in Prophecy

I would like to look at Revelation 13 and the beast rising out of the sea, having seven heads and ten horns. This beast has ten heads just like the dragon. But with this beast, the ten horns have crowns upon them, while the dragon has the crowns on the seven heads. "The ten crowns of the beast express his rule over a group of ten nations" (*Enduring Word Bible Commentary* on Revelation 13). This beast is like the fourth beast in Daniel 7:7—"It devoured and crushed and trampled down the remainder with its feet; and it was different from all the beasts that were before it, *and it had ten horns*." Like the dragon, which also has ten horns, the beast of the sea has ten horns. These both represent Rome, which is the fourth empire of Daniel's four beasts.

Now just as we stated before these are the two legs of iron in Daniels's image, the dragon is imperial Rome and the beast from the sea Papal Rome or the Holy Roman Empire.

But the dragon, gives his throne or crown to the beast (Revelation 13:2). This is what happened when imperial Rome gave its power to papal Rome by moving to Constantinople. The popes took up residency in Rome and so we have the transition from one iron leg to the other. But they are both the sixth head.

The five empires that had fallen when John wrote Revelation were Egypt, Assyria, Babylon, Medio-Persia, and Greece. Rome, then, is the

Wayne Grant

sixth empire, or head, and the one that now is, according to John. The other iron leg is the continuation of Rome and the sixth head. But the seventh head had not yet come. This empire as we said is the beast of the earth, America. Papal Rome or the Holy Roman Empire came to end just when the land beast was emerging.

We need to understand one other point so that we can understand who the seventh head of the dragon represents, and that is to know how the beast empire emerged. The beast was given his throne, power, and great authority by the dragon. Revelation 13:2 says,

> And the beast which I was like a like a *leopard*, and his feet were like those of *a bear*, and his mouth like the mouth of *a lion*. And the *dragon* gave him his power and his throne and great authority. (italics mine)

Notice that the beast from the sea which we have said is Papal Rome is only like the other four beasts in Daniel 7:1ff but is not one of them. This is because Papal Rome receives its throne from the dragon, the fourth kingdom, imperial Rome. The beast is just the other leg of iron. But it is still the sixth head even though there are two iron legs.

John in Revelation 12,13 and 17 has given us the clear picture from the image or statue in Daniel two of the head of gold, arms of silver, torso of bronze, legs of iron and feet of iron and clay. The four kingdoms in Daniel are Babylon, Medio-Persia, Greece and Rome. The dragon is identical to the sea beast and therefore represent the legs of iron, Imperial and Papal Rome. Each last for a thousand years and both are iron. In 1805 the second leg, the Holy Roman Empire ends and this is the end of the sixth head or empire.

Now according to Revelation 13:11, the beast of the sea is followed by the beast from the earth. This is America, the seventh head. America arises just as the Holy Roman Empire ends in 1805 and the popes lose temporal power in 1798. Napoleon inflicts the deadly wound which is later healed.

Now the seventh head is of the same kind as the other heads even as the beast from the earth is another of the same kind as the sea beast. United States is that new nation which would continue for a short time in comparison to Rome which was nearly two millennia. The United States is also a world empire. While America began in a remote part of the world and rather insignificant it has become a world empire with military bases in over 800 countries of the world. (Wikipedia: US military bases). America is lamb-like in appearance but inwardly speaks like a dragon. Therefore, she too is a beast and is like all the others. This is the daughter of Babylon.

Jeremiah 50:12 says *of* Babylon, "Your mother shall be sore confounded; she that bare you shall be ashamed: behold, the hindermost of the nations shall be a wilderness, a dry land, and a desert (KJV). *Hindermost* is from the Hebrew אחרית and means latter part, end, last. America is the last of the nations and the last in succession, when we consider the seven heads. But who is her mother? Rome is her mother. Twice, the Babylon of Jeremiah 50 and 51 is called the daughter of Babylon.

> The daughter of Babylon is like a threshing floor, at the time of treading it shall be stamped firm; yet in a little while the time of harvest will come for her. (Jeremiah 51:33)

> And they ride on horses marshalled like a man for the battle against you O daughter of Babylon. (Jeremiah 50:42)

Revelation 17:5 calls Babylon the mother of harlots and of the abominations of the earth. Here, we have Rome, not Britain, as the true mother of America. For this reason, she is called the daughter of Babylon. This lines up with Zechariah 5:8, where this woman inside an ephah is lifted up and carried to the land of Shinar, where she is set on her own pedestal, and a house is built for her. This is America, the daughter of Babylon. Babylon is called a city but is really a commercial empire destroyed in Revelation 18. She becomes a great merchant nation with whom the merchants of the earth are made rich. But Jeremiah 50–51 and Revelation 18 say she will be destroyed by fire. This will be a complete destruction, with no inhabitants left.

She must be the beast from the earth, who has two horns like a lamb but speaks like a dragon. She comes out of the earth, or the new world, which was uninhabited. She is a democratic republic, meaning she has both an elected Senate and an elected House of Representatives—two horns of power. She is lamb-like, in that she is founded on Christian principles, but like Papal Rome her religion is only outward. America, like imperial Rome before her, has become the hammer of the whole earth. Jeremiah 50:23 says, "How is the hammer of the whole earth cut asunder and broken! How is Babylon become a desolation among the nations!" (KJV).

The second beast is another of the same kind as the first beast, Rome, but is a different head. She is the daughter of Babylon. America is the final great empire on the earth. America has come to power only since World War II, a short time when compared to Rome, ancient Babylon, Assyria, Egypt, Greece, or Medio-Persia. America is the seventh head—less than 250 years, if you count from 1776.

Now this entire picture becomes clear when we look at Revelation 17 where just before her judgment the daughter of Babylon is seen riding the scarlet beast. This woman and the beast are the two beasts of Revelation 13. This is the iron and the clay in the feet of the image in Daniel two.

If you doubt this look briefly at Psalm 137:7,8 which I mentioned before. "Remember, O Lord, the children of Edom in the day of Jerusalem; who said, Rase it, rase it, even to the foundation thereof. O daughter of Babylon, who art to be destroyed; happy shall he be, that rewardeth thee as thou hast served us." Edom means red and this is the scarlet beast. The daughter of Babylon is the woman who rides him. These are the two beast of Revelation 13 joined together like the iron and the clay in the feet of Daniel's image. John has deliberately left this image of the woman and the beast until last, just when she is to be judged as recorded in Revelation 18 when in one day she is destroyed. It cannot get any plainer than this.

While the beast from the earth is called the false prophet in Revelation 19, we must also remember that Satan is called the dragon and the beast of the sea, antichrist, so they are also kingdoms.

Jeremiah 50:45 says, "Therefore hear the plan of the Lord which He has planned against Babylon, and His purposes which He has purposed against the land of the Chaldeans." Here is the daughter of Babylon. Then, in Isaiah 14:24–26 speaking about the scarlet beast.

> The Lord of hosts has sworn saying, Surely just as I have intended so it has happened and just as I have planned so it will stand, to break Assyria in My land and I will trample him on My mountains … This is the plan devised against the whole earth; and this is the hand that is stretched out against all the nations. For the Lord of hosts has planned and who can frustrate it?

God will trample down Assyria in His own land. This is the beast, the little horn, Antichrist, who is also the eighth. Here is God's plan to destroy antichrist in the land of Israel and America in her own land.

Gaebelein's comments on Zechariah 5 is a good source for the insight we need at this time. The first point Gaebelein makes is that this is the seventh vision of Zechariah. Here is some of his commentary:

> Zechariah 5:5–11. The angel commands the prophet to lift up his eyes to behold another startling vision. What are the leading figures in the vision? An ephah--which is a Jewish measure standing here for *commerce*. The eyes of all the land (or earth) are upon it. Commercialism is very prominent in Revelation in connection with the full measure of wickedness, the climax of ungodliness. In Revelation 18:1–24 merchants are mentioned who have grown rich through the abundance of her delicacies. Then the merchants are seen weeping, for no man buys their merchandise any more. And then a long list follows, including all the articles of modern commerce. Compare this with the awful description of the last times in James 5:1–20. Rich men are commanded to weep and howl, for miseries are come upon them. They heaped treasure together for the last days, and it was a heaping together by fraud, dishonesty in keeping back the hire of the laborers. They lived in pleasure (luxuriously) and

were wanton. Indeed, here is that burning question of the day, capital and labor, and its final outcome, misery and judgment upon commercialism, riches heaped up, and all in wickedness. In Habakkuk 2:12 the woe of judgment of that coming glory of the Lord is pronounced upon him that buildeth a town with blood and established a city by iniquity! The people are seen laboring for the fire and wearying themselves for vanity. Luxuries increase, riches, etc., are mentioned in the second and third chapters of Isaiah, chapters of judgment. Other passages could be quoted, but these are sufficient for our purpose. They show us that the climax of wickedness as it is in the earth when judgment will come, and Israel's time commences once more, will be connected with commerce, riches and luxuries. The ephah points to this. (Gaebelein: 1911, 135)

Here are some points we can make from this discussion. The first point is that this is the seventh vision of Zechariah. Next, the sixth vision was one of judgment. Therefore, like John in Revelation 17:1, the woman is revealed just before her judgment. The seventh vision is part of the vision of commercial Babylon. Also, the ephah, a symbol of commerce, represents commercial Babylon, as in Revelation 18, where the merchants stand far off because of the smoke of her burning. Next, this woman in the ephah is carried away by two women with the wings of a stork (unclean bird) to *the land of Shinar*. In Genesis 10:10 the kingdom of Babylon was in the land of Shinar.

Commercial Babylon is the one spoken of in Revelation 18. She is great in wealth, and all the merchants of the earth wail over her. All her music will be no more either. "And the ten horns and the beast will hate the harlot and will make her desolate and naked and will eat her flesh and will burn her up with fire." (Rev. 17:16) But as we said earlier, this is not at Christ's coming but before the rapture.

America is the beast from the earth, the seventh head and the last empire, which John foresees as about to be destroyed. This is the woman, Babylon riding the scarlet beast. The scarlet beast is the eighth head which was healed. This is the revived Roman Empire. These are the ten kings who are about to receive power one hour with the beast. This scarlet beast is still Rome.

The scarlet beast as we have said is the iron in the feet of the image of Daniel. This beast is an eighth because it arose after America the seventh head. After the popes regained his temporal power in 1929, the deadly wound healed, he began to build this new European Union, with the European Common market commencing in 1957. This is like the building of the tower of Babel which Nimrod the mighty hunter began in defiance of God. This is the kingdom of the beast and has ten horns as the feet of the image has ten toes. Today we have an economic merger taking place between the central banks of the G7 and the EU. Whenever these leaders of the countries they represent meet there is always eight members. The EU is the eighth. This makes me think of the seven heads and ten horns of the scarlet beast.

The European Union came in as an eighth.

> The President of the European Commission has attended since he was first invited to the third G7 summit in 1977, Roy Jenkins was the then-President. Since 1981 the President has attended all sessions of the G7. The EU is currently represented by the Commission President and the President of the European Council. (Wikipedia, "G7 summit meetings")

I believe that this present union of the G7 and the EU may represent the seven heads and ten horns of the beast. This group has been meeting together since 1981, but every time they meet for a G7 summit, there are always eight representatives and eight separate flags. The reason is that the eighth leader is the head of the EU. The EU, then, is headed up by the beast with ten horns. The G7, likewise, is headed up by America, the woman. Here is the economic union and mark of the beast.

10

How Close Are We to the Final Week?

At the present time, how close are we to the final seven-year tribulation event? Or to be more precise, how close are we to the Second Coming of Christ? Let's focus on the Second Coming, rather than the tribulation. Jesus says, "Watch therefore: for you not know what hour your Lord is coming. But know this that if the head of the house had known in what watch the thief would come, he would have watched and would not have suffered his house to be broken into" (Matthew 24:42–43).

Jesus says no man knows the day or the hour of the coming of the Son of Man, not the angels, not even the Son but the Father alone. But the head of the house will know which watch of the night the thief is coming. (Matthew 24:43).

This is an important clue to the Second Coming of Christ. We cannot know the day or hour, but we can know the watch in the night. Christ the head of the house knows which watch of the night. Here, we must look at other scripture to understand what Jesus means by a watch in the night.

Moses says, "For a thousand years in Thy sight are like yesterday when it passes by, or as a watch in the night" (Psalm 90:4). Moses says that with God, a watch in the night is like a thousand years. Jesus says that the head of the house knows in which watch the thief is coming. I suggest, from other passages, that Jesus is talking about two thousand years, or the second watch, for the time of His Second Coming.

To understand this, we need to look at the parable of the Good Samaritan. Jesus says that when the Good Samaritan saw the man who fell among thieves, he felt compassion on him,

> and came to him and bandaged up his wounds pouring oil and wine on them and he put him on his own beast and brought him to an inn and took care of him. And on the next day he took out two denarii and gave them to the innkeeper and said, "Take care of him and whatever more you spend *when I return, I will repay you*." (Luke 10:34–35 italics mine)

Now that the good Samaritan is Christ, and the man who fell among thieves is Adam, Paul also seems to suggest, "For you know the grace of our Lord Jesus Christ that though He was rich yet for your sake He became pour that you through His poverty might become rich" (2 Corinthians 8:9). This is exactly what the Good Samaritan did by becoming poor so that the man who fell among thieves might become rich. Christ would return, and he would repay whatever more the cost was for this man.

The point is that Christ is coming back two days after He left because he gives the innkeeper two days wages to meet the expenses of his guest. I believe this is the second watch of the night, which Jesus said that the head of the house knows. Now we can also see it as the last three years of the tribulation and that Jesus is coming sometime in the third year. But for the sake of argument let's try to get an estimate as to exactly when Christ left earth to return to His Father.

We know that Christ was thirty years old when His ministry began (Luke 3:23) and that John mentions three Passovers, the last one when Jesus was crucified, making Him about thirty-three at His crucifixion. But when was Christ born? This is another unknown date and is exactly why we may know the year but not the exact time. However, most historians agree that Herod the Great died about 4 BC (Wikipedia, "Herod the Great"). This death of Herod is described in Josephus with the mention of a lunar eclipse in that year. There was a lunar eclipse in 4 BC, but there were two lunar eclipses in 1 BC as well. Herod's death could have been later, and so Jesus's birth could be later and, therefore, His ascension later.

This is the reason we must caution ourselves on picking dates. We simply do not know. Until we see the temple being built in Jerusalem, we are not in the final week of Daniel 9. Many have made the mistake of calculating dates, which later proved wrong.

> Every word of God is tested; He is a shield to those who take refuge in Him. Do not add to His words lest He reprove you, and you be proved a liar. (Proverbs 30:5–6)

Another important date is the seventieth week from Daniel 9:24. Sixty-nine of those weeks were fulfilled at the destruction of the temple in AD 70. The final week can only be fulfilled if Israel is back in the land. Also, Israel must control the temple mount and finally that the temple is rebuilt. So a covenant has to be made.

The Messiah was cut off *after sixty-two week*, according to Daniel 9:26, not sixty-nine weeks, as the dispensationalist try to say. Daniel 9:26 says, "Then *after the sixty-two weeks the Messiah will be cut off* and have nothing and the people of the prince who is to come will destroy the city and the sanctuary." (italics mine). But the city and the sanctuary were destroyed seven weeks of years later in AD 70 (Wikipedia, "Siege of Jerusalem [70 CE]"). The sixty-ninth week, then, is AD 70, not when Messiah is cut off, for that takes place after sixty-two weeks.

Therefore, the seven-year tribulation week begins not with Second Coming of Christ, as dispensationalists claim, but with *the rebuilding of the temple*, as the succession of weeks stopped when the temple was destroyed around AD 70. Yet we need to be cautious on dates and so until we see the temple built in Jerusalem we are not into the final week.

I hope these ideas will help you prepare and persevere until the end. If you do not know Christ as your Lord and Savior don't wait but receive Him into your heart today so that whether you live or die you may be with the Lord.

Meanwhile what shall we do? I will tell you what we should do. God tell it on the mountains, over the hills and everywhere, go tell it on the mountains that Jesus Christ is born.

Now here is a verse supporting the post-tribulation position. Revelation 20:4,

> "And I saw thrones and they sat upon them and judgment was given to them. And I saw the souls of those who had been beheaded because of the testimony of Jesus and because of the word of God, and those who had not worshiped the beast or his image, and had not received the mark upon their hand; and they came to life and reigned with Christ for a thousand years."

Now these came to life after the tribulation. This is the first resurrection which begins the millennium. Therefore, these are the church of Christ since they will rise and reign with Christ for a thousand years. Dispensationalism places tribulation saints outside the church.

This verse needs to be compared with Revelation 15:2, "And I saw, as it were, a sea of glass mixed with fire, and those who had come off victorious from the beast and from his image and from the number of his name standing on the sea of glass, holding harps of God."

This persecution is described in Revelation 13:5-7

> "And there was given to him a mouth speaking arrogant words and blasphemes; and authority to act for forty-two months was given to him. And he opened his mouth in blasphemies against God, to blaspheme His name and His tabernacle, that is, those who dwell in heaven. And it was given to him to make war with the saints and to overcome them; and authority over every tribe and people and tongue and nation was given to him"

The forty-two months is foreshadowed in the taunting of Goliath where he taunts the armies of Israel for forty days. Then in 1 Samuel 17:17 we read,

"Then Jesse said to David his son, "Take now for your brothers an ephah of this roasted grain and these ten loaves, and run to the camp to your brothers...v.20 So David arose early in the morning and left the flock with a keeper and took the supplies and went as Jesse had commanded him."

Only the Father knows the day or the hour. Not the angels nor even the Son. This was the forty second day when David went down to the battle at the commandment of his father Jesse and killed the beast. Although we cannot know the day or the hour it does seem we can know the month when Christ will return. For this reason, John has recorded the last three and a half years in months and not days. The doctrine of imminency would exclude such knowledge.

11

The Feast of Tabernacles

In conclusion, one other important time line, which we mentioned at the beginning, is the Feast of Tabernacles. This is the final feast in the Jewish festival year. This feast lasts seven days and celebrates the end of the harvest and commemoration of the wandering and living in tents. The feast is in the seventh month, lasts seven days, and ends on the seventh day. On the eighth day, there is a rest.

In the Gospel of John, we read, concerning this feast,

> Now the feast of the Jews the feast of Booths was at hand. His brothers therefore said to Him, "Depart from here, and go into Judea, that Your disciples also may behold Your works which You are doing. For no one does anything in secret, when he himself seeks to be know publicly. If You, do these things, *show Yourself to the world*." For not even His brothers were believing in Him. Jesus therefore said to them, "My time is not yet at hand; but your time is always ready. The world cannot hate you; but it hates Me, because I testify of it, that its deeds are evil. Go up to the feast yourselves; *I do not go up to this feast because My time has not yet fully come*."
> (John 7:2–8 italics mine)

The feast to which Jesus must go is the Feast of Passover, in order to die. The Feast of Tabernacles was to be fulfilled later, when He revealed Himself to the world. This last feast would happen at His advent.

> Now on the last day, the great day of the feast, Jesus stood and cried out saying, "If any man is thirsty let him come to Me and drink." (John 7:37)

The last day of the Feast of Tabernacles is when Jesus appears. This is the eighth day, according to Leviticus:

> On the first day is a holy convocation; you shall do no laborious work of any kind. For seven days you shall present an offering *by fire* to the Lord. On the eighth day you shall have a holy convocation and present an offering *by fire* to the Lord; it is an assembly. You shall do no laborious work. (Leviticus 23:35)

This day is called the great day in John 7:37; that is, the eighth day, a holy convocation. Here, we have a picture of Christ revealing Himself after the final week. This must be His Second Coming. *"For seven days you shall present an offering by fire"* (Leviticus 23:36). This fire could represent the tribulation. At the end of it, Christ shall appear, just as John presents it in chapter 7 of his gospel.

This feast of seven days, then, the last feast in the Jewish year, must be the tribulation week, at the end of which Jesus will stand on the Mount of Olives at His advent. Then, with our tents changed into new bodies, we all shall come down and enter Jerusalem with everlasting joy upon our heads.

> And the redeemed of the Lord will return, and come with joyful shouting to Zion, with everlasting joy upon their heads. They will find gladness and joy, and sorrow and sighing will flee away. (Isaiah 35:10)

Not long now. Maranatha! As the Feast of Tabernacles is the final feast, and the first two involved the church, then so must the last feast involve the church of Christ. Paul, speaking to the Corinthians, says, "Let us therefore celebrate the feast, not with old leaven, nor with the leaven of malice and wickedness, but with the unleavened bread of sincerity and truth." (1 Corinthians 5:8). Here, we see the church participating in the Feast of Unleavened Bread.

Again, with reference to our fellowship in the Passover meal, Jesus says to His disciples,

> Truly, truly, I say to you, unless you eat the flesh of the Son of Man and drink His blood you have no life in yourselves. He who eats My flesh and drinks My blood has eternal life, and I will raise him up on the last day. (John 6:53)

We all must participate in the Passover of Christ in order to have eternal life.

> I have been crucified with Christ and it is no longer I who lives but Christ lives in me and the life which I now live in the flesh I live by faith in the Son of God who loved me and delivered Himself up for me. (Galatians 2:20)

The same is true of Pentecost, for Paul says in 1 Corinthians 12:13, "For by one Spirit we were all baptized into one body, whether Jews or Greeks, whether slaves or free, and we were all made to drink of one Spirit." This is our participation in the outpouring of the Spirit at Pentecost, and there are no exceptions, whether Jew or Greek.

Likewise, there is no exception in our participation in the Feast of Tabernacles. The three feasts were mandatory for all Israel, and they also were spiritual. The feasts are prophetic of the work of Christ and our participation in it, and since the first two involved all Christians, so too must the Feast of Tabernacles. The idea that the church will be removed before the completion of the Feast of Tabernacles seems contrary to scripture. For this reason, I believe that the pretribulation rapture scenario is incorrect.

You shall dwell in booths for seven days; all the native-born in Israel shall live in booths. (Leviticus 23:42).

Paul says,

For we know that if the earthly tent which is our home is torn down, we have a building from God, a house not made with hands, eternal in the heavens. (2 Corinthians 5:1)

The Greek word for *tent* is σκηνη; it is the noun form of the verb σκηνοω, used by John:

And the Word became flesh and *dwelt* among us and we beheld His glory, glory as an only begotten from the Father full of grace and truth. (John 1:14 italics mine)

This means *to tabernacle* among us, in a body of flesh. Like Christ, we too must dwell in tents. For us, though, we must remain in tents until the end. How, then, can we receive our new bodies before the feast is ended? Jesus says, the one who believes in Me, I will raise up on the last day. Not the first day; it was the last day of the Feast of Tabernacles, which was the eighth, that Jesus revealed Himself to the world. After the feast, the people went back to living in buildings. In My Father's house, Jesus said, there are many mansions. He has gone to prepare a place for us. When Jesus returns, we shall enter our permanent dwelling place. This is the rapture. But before that day, we must offer a sacrifice of fire for seven days. This is the seven-year tribulation period. Futurism is as true as historicism, and neither can exclude the other.

At the Feast of Tabernacles, water was drawn from the pool of Siloam every day and brought up to the altar, where it was poured out. But on the seventh day, *this ritual* was repeated seven times. John 7:39 equates this with the pouring out of the Holy Spirit. This already took place at the Pentecost, the Feast of Weeks. The church has received the Holy Spirit. The pouring out of the water at the Feast of Tabernacles is prophetic of God's pouring out His Spirit on the house of Israel during the tribulation period. This is yet to come. This ritual of the water is not part of the feast itself but was added to commemorate the water given in the wilderness and the prayer for rain in the dry season. In other words, the ritual did not apply so much to the church as to Israel's coming to Christ. The feast, however, applies to the church, as we have demonstrated.

> "And I will not hide My face from them any longer, for
> I shall have poured out My Spirit on the house of Israel"
> declares the Lord God. (Ezekiel 39:29).

Jesus reveals Himself on the last day of the feast to the Jews, having already poured out His Spirit on the house of Israel. The account of this pouring out of the Holy Spirit on the house of Israel, the Jews, is recorded in Ezekiel 37, with the vision of the valley of dry bones. This takes place through the ministry of the two witnesses in Revelation 11.

This is when, according to Paul,

> And thus all Israel will be saved just as it is written,
> "The Deliverer will come from Zion He will remove
> ungodliness from Jacob. And this is My covenant with
> them when I take away their sins." (Romans 11:26)

> And I will pour out on the house of David and on the
> inhabitants of Jerusalem the Spirit of grace and of
> supplication so that they will look on Me whom they have
> pierced; and they will mourn for Him, as one mourns
> for an only son, and they weep bitterly over Him, like
> the bitter weeping over a first-born. (Zechariah 12:10)

Isaiah 44:3 says the same thing: "For I will pour out water on the thirsty land and streams on the dry ground; I will pour out My Spirit on your offspring, and My blessing on your descendants."

Then, likewise:

> Until the Spirit is poured out upon us from on high, And
> the wilderness becomes a fertile field, And the fertile
> field is considered as a forest. Then justice will dwell

> in the wilderness, and righteousness will abide in the
> fertile field ... then My people will live in a peaceful
> habitation, and in secure dwellings and in undisturbed
> resting places. (Isaiah 32:15–16, 18)

The Feast of Tabernacles was a dry time of year, when the harvest of the fruit trees took place. So too this pouring out of water on the rock of the altar was the pouring out of water on the thirsty land, and by this water, the wilderness was transformed into a fertile field. Israel, as a nation, was a dry land without water for two thousand years after their rejection of Messiah.

The dry bones were very dry, according to Ezekiel 37:2 and therefore must have been dry for a long time. They did not receive the life Jesus came to give them. But the Spirit will be poured out on them. And these dry bones will come to life in a great awakening, like Gideon's fleece was dry while the ground all around it was wet, to symbolize the Spirit going to the Gentiles, while Israel, like the older son, missed out on the festivities. But according to these scriptures, this indeed will change during the Feast of Tabernacles before the end of the age. This feast, they will not miss.

The church of Christ has participated in the first two feasts and will participate in the Feast of Tabernacles as well. However, we already have the Holy Spirit, just as the book of Acts says. When the Jews turn to Christ, they too will be saved, receive the Holy Spirit, and become part of the body of Christ. They will enter into the new covenant and will join in the festivities. Dispensationalism has made clear the distinction between the church as the body of Christ and the nation of Israel, the Jews who are still, as a whole, separate.

But this division will soon be no more, for according to Paul, we are already fellow heirs and fellow members of the body and fellow partakers of the promise in Christ Jesus through the gospel. (Ephesians 3:6). Israel, as a nation, has just not entered into the church, the body of Christ. For Paul says, "For by one Spirit we were all baptized into one body, whether Jews or Greeks, whether slaves or free, and we were all made to drink of one Spirit" (1 Corinthians 12:13). But since the Spirit is given through faith, Israel, not believing in Christ as their Messiah are still outside the church. When the Spirit is poured out on the house of Israel, then they will be baptized into the body of Christ, even as we were. Praise God.

The two groups are clearly seen in Revelation 14 and 15. The 144,000 are standing on Mount Zion, and the great multitude are standing upon the sea of glass. This is the church of God, fellow heirs and fellow members of the body.

Finally, then, all these things are irrelevant, if we do not know Christ, whom to know is to have eternal life. If you find yourself outside the blessings of God in Christ, then I have good news for you. You are only a prayer away.

> If you confess with your mouth that Jesus is Lord and believe in your heart that God raised Him from the dead you will be saved. (Romans 10:9)

> For whoever will call upon the name of the Lord will be saved. (Romans 10:13)

> Behold I stand at the door and knock, if anyone hears My voice and opens the door, I will come into him and dine with him and he will dine with Me. (Revelation 3:20)

Justification is a free gift by His grace when we receive Christ. The redemption took place in Christ. Without Christ, we cannot have the forgiveness of our sins.

The four spiritual laws are still the same: (1) God loves you (John 3:16). (2) All have sinned (Romans 3:23). That means you and me. This sin has separated us from God (Isaiah 59:2). (3) Christ died for sins (Romans 5:8). When Christ died on the cross, it was for your sins. (4) You must receive Christ (John 1:12). When we admit to God in prayer that we are sinners and believe that Christ died for those sins and rose again for our justification, and we humbly ask Jesus to be our Lord and Savior, He will come into us and be born in us today. Salvation is the forgiveness of our sins through the cross of Christ.

When we receive Christ, we receive the remission of sins. Our spirits, which were dead in transgressions, come to life. What is born of the Spirit is spirit. This spirit is our new nature.

> For you have not received a spirit of slavery leading to fear again, but you have received a spirit of adoption whereby we cry Abba Father. (Romans 8:15).

Christ has become a life-giving spirit (1 Corinthians 15:45).

Galatians 2:20 says, "I have been crucified with Christ and it is no longer I who live but Christ lives in me and the life which I now live in the flesh I live by faith in the Son of God who loved me and delivered Himself up for me."

Galatians 4:6 confirms this transaction: "And because you are sons, God has sent forth the Spirit of His Son into our hearts crying Abba, Father." When we receive Christ as our Savior, we *receive* our adoption as sons (Galatians 4:5).

Second Corinthians 5:17 says, "If any man is in Christ, he is a new creation, old things have passed away, behold all things are new." The new creation comes through the gospel.

The Greek word in Galatians 4:5 is απολαμβανω—"to receive back." This suggests something we had before but lost. The same word is used of the receiving back of the prodigal son by the Father in Luke 15:27. When Adam sinned, he lost this original sonship. He became a slave of sin when he received the forbidden fruit. Adoption is how we are sons again. And as Paul says in Galatians 4:6, because *you are sons* by adoption, God will send forth the Spirit of Christ into our hearts, crying ABBA Father. When we receive Christ, we receive a new heart. Then, God will send forth the Spirit into our new hearts. This is the promise of the Holy Spirit by faith. Both are there, or neither are there. Faith alone.

This is the *new heart* and *new spirit* that God promises in the new covenant to those who believe in His Son. (See Ezekiel 36:26–27; also, John 3:5.)

The next thing we expect to appear is the white horse of the Apocalypse. But the living creatures say to John, "Come and see!" This is something already historical but needs spiritual eyes to see. This is

Antichrist, who already is sitting in the church of God, if, as we suspect, the final week may begin as early as 2021. The rider of the white horse, who has a bow, must be the pope. He has been riding around the world in his white garment as the world's peacemaker and in his popemobile for some time. This is not a peace with God, though, but a common unity of all faiths under Rome. As the seventieth week has to do with Israel, then the white-horse deception must begin with Israel. Next year, we may see the peace agreement between the Vatican and Israel. This seems more like the ecumenical movement bringing all faiths together in Jerusalem. The Jews will submit to this in order to have the right to a new temple, where they can practice Judaism according to the Mosaic Law—with sacrifices.

In Daniel 9:27, the Roman prince makes a covenant with the many for one week, but in the middle of the week, *he puts a stop to the daily sacrifice* and sets up the abomination of desolation. (See Matthew 24:15.) Time will tell. Until then, let's keep watching and waiting, as our Lord commanded us.

> And be like men who are waiting for their master when he returns from the wedding feast, so that they may immediately open the door to him when he comes and knocks. Blessed are those slaves whom the master shall find *on the alert* when he comes; truly I say to you that he will gird himself to serve and have them recline at table and will come up and wait on them. (Luke 12:36–37)

Beloved, we must be on the alert and patiently wait for the return of Christ.

To recline at this table is to be at the marriage supper of the Lamb (Revelation 19:7–10). To be on the alert is important because our adversary, the devil, prowls around like a roaring lion, seeking whom he may devour, whom resist, firm in the faith.

"AFTERWORD"

Heavens Declare His Glory

The end of the age is declared in scripture, as we have demonstrated from various texts. But the end of the age is also *declared in the heavens.*

> The heavens are declaring the glory of God; and their expanse is declaring the work of His hands. Day to day pours forth speech, and night to night reveals knowledge. There is no speech nor are there words where their voice is not heard. Their line has gone out through all the earth. And their utterances to the end of the world. In them He has placed a tent for the sun which is as a bridegroom coming out of his chamber; It rejoices as a strong man to run his course. Its rising is from one end of the heavens, and its circuit to the other end of them; And there is nothing hidden from its heat. (Psalm 19:1-6)

The heavens of which David is speaking refers to the course of the sun throughout the year, as it makes its way through the various constellations of the zodiac. The twelve constellations are the tent, where the sun dwells throughout the year as it travels from one constellation, or house, to the next. David also compares the sun to a bridegroom who leaves from one point and returns to where he left. While this is true of the sun in the sky, it is also a picture of Christ, our true bridegroom, and the great light, who has come, and tabernacle among us, only to return to heaven until the time of His Second Coming at the end of the age.

This is where we must know some church history in order to understand the picture clearly. Tertullian and Augustine, to mention just two, stated that Christ was born on December 25, and this fact was written down in the archives at Rome for all to observe (Rolleston 1862, 130). Not until the archives were destroyed at the fall of Rome in 476 did the fact of the time when Jesus was born ever come into question.

This date is important for understanding the psalmist because it is not known exactly which constellation marks the beginning, when the bridegroom comes out of his chamber. In other words, at which constellation do you start, as the path of the sun is circular? Some believed you start with Virgo because Jesus was born of a virgin, but this is not where we should start.

We should start with Capricorn because on December 25, two thousand years ago, the sun was just about to leave the constellation of Capricorn. Paul says, "But when the fulness of time came, *God sent forth His Son* born of a woman born under the Law" (Galatians 4:4 italics mine). God's timing is perfect. It was then that John 1:14 came about: "And the Word became flesh and *dwelt* among us and we beheld His glory, glory as an only begotten from the Father, full of grace and truth."

Also, Jesus's statement in John 10:36—"Do you say of Him whom the Father sanctified and *sent into the world*, you are blaspheming because I said, I am the Son of God"—takes on new meaning when we consider the context of that statement as the Feast of Dedication, always on Kislev 25 (John 10:22).

Therefore, believing church history that Jesus was born on December 25, we will take Capricorn as the beginning, when the bridegroom comes out of his chamber, and the constellation of Sagittarius as the end. The twelve constellations may be equated to twelve hours in a day. When questioned about His returning to Judea and the threat of the Jews, Jesus said:

> Are there not twelve hours in the day? If anyone walks in the day, he does not stumble because he sees the light of the world. But if anyone walks in the night he stumbles because the light is not in him. (John 11:9–10)

Antichrist comes at the last hour, according to 1 John 2:18. This is also called the night. What is interesting is that the last constellation before Sagittarius is Scorpio. Out of the twelve signs, the scorpion is the only deadly creature of the zodiac. Jesus said, "Have I not chosen twelve of you and yet one is a devil?" This was Judas, and he is the prototype of the Antichrist. The sun then travels all through the constellation, but just before the end, it must travel through Scorpio.

Jesus kept saying to His disciples that His hour had not yet come and told them to work while it is day, for the night is coming when no man can work. Then, when that hour came, Jesus was betrayed and put to death. The night is when the sun sets. Just as Jesus went through that hour as the bridegroom, so will His body, the church. This eleventh hour is what I have warned about in this book.

Just before the Second Coming of Christ, symbolized in the constellation of Sagittarius—one of the most luminous of the constellations—the scorpion comes up, at the last hour. Interesting too is that the sun is in Scorpio for *only seven days*, due to precession. Scorpio, over the last six thousand years, has nearly dropped from the path of the sun (Chartrand 1990, 184 italics mine).

Speaking of the seed of the woman, Genesis says, "He shall bruise you on the head but you shall bruise him on the head." (Genesis 3:15). The heel wound happened at the cross, but the head wound is about to come at the second coming of Christ. Like David striking Goliath on the head with a stone.

Yes, indeed, the heavens declare the Second Coming of Christ, and it is after the night, just as we have stated in the book.

REFERENCES

Aland, B., K. Aland, J. Karavidopoulos, C.M. Martini, and B. Metzger, eds. 1983. *The Greek New Testament*. United Bible Society.

Ante-Nicene Fathers ed., by Alexander Roberts and James Donaldson. (Peabody Mass: Hendrickson Publishers, 1995) Vol 7, p. 382.

Bainton Roland H., *Here I Stand: A Life of Martin Luther* (Nashville: Abingdon Press, 1991)

Benedict XV, Litterae Apostolicae, *Inter Sodalicia*, March 22, 1918, AAS 10, 1918, 182:

Blasphemous Roman Catholic Church Statements, "On the Authority of Councils" book 2 chapter 17. https://thechristianlife.com/blasphemous-ro

Carruthers, S. W., ed. 1946. *The Confession of Faith of the Assembly of Divines at Westminster*. London: Publishing Office of the Presbyterian Church of England.

Catholic Truth Society (Great Britain). *Publications of the Catholic Truth Society* 29: 11. Ulan Press: 2012. Quotes from Cardinal Sarto.1896.

Chartrand, M. R. 1990. *SKYGUIDE: A Field Guide to the Heavens*. New York: Golden Press.

Dowling, J. 1871. *The History of Romanism*. New York: E. Walker.

Elliot, Edward B. *Commentary on the Apocalypse.* (London: Seeley Jackson and Halliday. 1851) Vol 3

Foxes Book of Martyrs by John Foxe, ed., Harold J. Chadwick. (Florida: Bridge-Logos, 2001)

Gaebelein, Arno Clemens, 1861-1945: Studies in Zechariah. New York: Francis E. Fitch, 1911.

Grattan, Henry. 1887. *Romanism and the Reformation: From the Standpoint of Prophecy.* Hodder and Stoughton. Harvard University.

Guizik, David. Online. "Enduring Word Bible Commentary on Revelation 13." https://enduringword.com/bible-commentary/revelation-13. Accessed March 2020.

Hislop, Alexander. 1916. *The Two Babylons.* England: A&C Black.

Hunt, Dave. 1994. *A Woman Rides the Beast.* Oregon: Harvest House Publishers.

Josephus. 1987. *The Works of Flavius Josephus.* Translated by A. M. William Whiston. Peabody MA: Hendrickson Publishers.

Lenski, R. C. H. 1946. *The Interpretation of St. Paul's Epistles to the Colossians, to the Thessalonians, to Timothy, to Titus and to Philemon.* Minneapolis, Min: Augsburg Publishing House.

Moulton and Milligan. 1997. *Vocabulary of the Greek Testament.* Peabody, MA: Hendrickson Publishers.

Mounce, William. 2009. *Basics of Biblical Greek Grammar.* Grand Rapids, MI: Zondervan.

Pope Pius V, quoted in Barclay, "Cities Petrus Bertanous," 218 https://www.christianityboard.com/threads/is-the

Praeclara gratulationis publicae—The Reunion of Christendom. 1894. Rome. https://www.papalencyclicals.net/leo13/l13pr

Rolleston, F. *MAZZAROTH*. Whitefish, Montana: Kessinger Publishing LLC, 2003

Snaith, N.H. 1992. *The Hebrew Bible*. London: British and Foreign Bible Society.

Strong, James. 1980. 4th ed. *The Exhaustive Concordance of the Bible*. Peabody, MA: Hendrickson.

The 1689 Baptist Confession of Faith, ed., Samuel E. Waldron. (Simpson Publishing Co. 1991). Ch. 26, IV.

Vine, W. E. 1984. *Vine's Complete Expository Dictionary of Old and New Testament Words*. Nashville: Thomas Nelson.

Westminster Confession of Faith. 1646. On the Church, chapter 25, VI. http://lmpc.org/wp-content/uploads/2013

Wiersbe, Warren. 1977. "Luther: The Methods and Fruits of Justification." In *Treasury of The Worlds Greatest Sermons*, (Grand Rapids MI: Kregel) 346-353

Wikipedia. 2020. "Amillennialism." Last modified October 18, 2020. https://en.wikipedia.org/wiki/Amillennialism#.

Wikipedia. 2020. "Francis II Holy Roman Emperor." Last modified December 13, 2020.

https://en.wikipedia.org/wiki/Francis_II,_Holy_

Wikipedia. 2020. "Francisco Ribera." Last modified May 19, 2020. https://en.wikipedia.org/wiki/Francisco_Ribera.

Wikipedia. 2020. "Grandville Sharp classical Grammarian." Last modified Dec. 7, 2020. https://en.wikipedia.org/wiki/Granville_Sharp.

Wikipedia. 2020. "John Nelson Darby." Last modified Dec. 6, 2020. https://en.wikipedia.org/wiki/John_Nelson_Darby.

Wikipedia. 2020. "Manuel De Lacunza." Last modified Dec. 14, 2020. https://en.wikipedia.org/wiki/Manuel_Lacunza.

Wikipedia. 2020. "Pontifex Maximus." Last modified Dec. 19, 2020. https://en.wikipedia.org/wiki/Pontifex_maximus.

Wikipedia. 2020. "Sennacherib." Last modified Dec. 19, 2020.

https://en.wikipedia.org/wiki/Sennacherib

Wikipedia. 2020. "Vicar of Christ." Last modified Dec. 13, 2020. https://en.wikipedia.org/wiki/Vicar_of_Christ.

04090012-00836138

Printed in the United States
By Bookmasters